Popular Mechanics

Garage
Makeovers

Adding Space Without Adding On

RICK PETERS

Hearst Books
A Division of Sterling Publishing Co., Inc.
New York

Note: The safety guards were removed for clarity in many of the photographs in this book. Make sure to always use all safety devices according to the manufacturers' instructions.

Producer Credits
Design: Sandy Freeman
Cover design: Celia Fuller
Contributing writer: Cheryl A. Romano
Photography: Christopher J. Vendetta
Cover photo: Gladiator GarageWorks by Whirlpool Corporation
Illustrations: Bob Crimi
Copy Editor: Barbara McIntosh Webb
Page layout: Sandy Freeman
Index: Nan Badgett

Safety Note: Homes built prior to 1978 may have been constructed with hazardous materials: lead and asbestos. You can test painted surfaces with a test kit available at most hardware stores. Asbestos can be found in ceiling and wall materials, joint compound, insulation, and flooring. Hire a professional, licensed hazardous-removal company to check for this, and remove any hazardous materials found.

Library of Congress Cataloging-in-Publication
Peters, Rick.
Popular mechanics garage makeovers. Adding space without adding on / Rick Peters.
p. cm.
Includes index.
ISBN-13: 978-1-58816-513-8
ISBN-10: 1-58816-513-2
1. Garages--Remodeling--Amateurs' manuals. 2. Storage in the home--Amateurs' manuals. I. Title: Adding space without adding on. II. Title.
TH4960.P478 2006
690'.898--dc22

2006007912

Published by Hearst Books
A Division of Sterling Publishing Co., Inc.
387 Park Avenue South, New York, NY 10016

Popular Mechanics and Hearst Books are trademarks of Hearst Communications, Inc.

www.popularmechanics.com

For information about custom editions, special sales, and premium and corporate purchases, please contact Sterling Special Sales Department at 800-805-5489 or specialsales@sterlingpub.com.

Distributed in Canada by Sterling Publishing
c/o Canadian Manda Group, 165 Dufferin Street
Toronto, Ontario, Canada M6K 3H6

Distributed in Australia by Capricorn Link (Australia) Pty. Ltd.
P.O. Box 704, Windsor, NSW 2756 Australia

Manufactured in China

Sterling ISBN 13: 978–1–58816–513–8
ISBN 10: 1–58816–513–2

Acknowledgments

For all their help, advice, and support, I offer special thanks to:

Nora DePalma for Decorative Panels International (DPI), for supplying their snazzy metallic pegboard panels used in the Mechanic's Dream makeover.

Mischel Schonberg at Clopay, for providing the superbly crafted and great-looking garage door installed for the carport conversion makeover.

Elina Gorlenkova with Armstrong Ceilings, for providing their Washable White acoustical ceiling tiles used in the new living space makeover.

Kevin Shaha at Racor, Inc., for supplying their InterChange line of wall-mounted hangers used in the workshop makeover.

Don Sneed of Better Living Technologies, LLC, for the extremely wear-resistant and good-looking G-Floor they provided for the workshop makeover.

Susan Stroup at Snap Lock Industries for RaceDeck, for dressing up our Mechanic's Dream makeover with their hard-working, easy-to-install, colorful modular flooring.

Charlene Leonard at The Chamberlain Group, Inc., for providing their Whisper Drive belt-driven garage door opener used in the carport conversion makeover.

Michele Savalox of Gladiator GarageWorks, for supplying their well-made and super-flexible GearWall panels and accessories used in the workshop makeover.

Doug Miller of Sauder, for Hot Rod Garage by Sauder, for providing their stout but attractive cabinets used in the Mechanic's Dream makeover.

Mark Kelly of Grid Iron, for dressing up our living space makeover with their industrial-quality wall panels and accessories.

Lynn Kaperak-Miller at Rubbermaid Home Products, for supplying their FastTrack system and cabinets, which formed the heart of our All About Storage makeover.

Keith Wiethe at Kronotex USA, for providing their easy-to-install and durable laminate flooring used in the craft room makeover.

Rick Chamberlain of storeWALL, for supplying their sturdy and attractive wall organization panels used in the craft room makeover.

Rick Gumpert at The Accessories Group, for providing the wall accessories used to organize the craft room makeover.

Terry Palermo of Triton Products, for supplying their nifty pegboard fastening system and pegboard accessories used in the Mechanic's Dream makeover.

Jim Stinner at Rust-Oleum, for providing the durable and good-looking epoxy coating system that we used in the All About Storage makeover.

Christopher Vendetta, for taking great photographs under less-than-desirable conditions and under tight deadlines.

Bob Crimi, for superb illustrations.

Sandy Freeman, whose design and page layout talents are evident on every page of this book.

Barb Webb, copyediting whiz, for ferreting out mistakes and gently suggesting corrections.

Heartfelt thanks to my constant inspiration: Cheryl, Lynne, Will, and Beth.

Contents

Introduction

Cruise around any neighborhood and look into an open garage. What do you see? A mess, right? Piles of boxes, lawn equipment, sporting gear, bicycles, you name it. Sometimes you'll even see a car in there! Why do so many garages look like the aftermath of a tornado? Because they're pressed into service for so many different roles. In addition to occasionally storing a car or cars, most garages are called on to shelter a workshop, household storage, lawn equipment, a craft area, a play space, and even a laundry room.

How can you reclaim your garage and maximize your space? You're holding the answer in your hands. *Garage Makeovers* is all about taking back control of your garage and shaping it into a functional space, whether it be a workshop, craft room, or living space.

In these pages, you'll see how we took an actual carport, converted it into a garage, and then made over the garage in five of the most frequently requested themes: a Mechanic's Dream, a Craft Room, a Workshop, a new Living Space, and one makeover that's devoted solely to Storage. This novel approach shows you what kinds of upgrades and renovations might inspire your project. Whatever your own makeover plans, we hope you can find a compatible style and project in these pages...something that makes you say, "That's what I want!"

To help you reach your makeover goals, the book is divided into three parts. The "Planning a Makeover" section includes the fundamentals on which you'll base your new look. In "Real Makeover Examples," you'll see the real-life garages and six makeovers. And in "Creating a New Look," you'll go step-by-step through the basics that let you actually do the projects yourself.

We hope you park yourself here for a while, and enjoy getting the inspiration and information for your "new" garage.

—James Meigs
Editor-in-Chief, *Popular Mechanics*

Planning Your Makeover

The first recorded instance of the word "garage" in English was in 1902. Probably that same year, newfangled horseless carriages started sharing their spaces with bicycles-built-for-two, canning supplies, and coal chutes. Today, what we cram into our garages has changed, but the need to make better use of the space remains. In this section, we'll help you plan what needs to be done and how to make it happen.

Step by step, we'll take you through the basics: garage design, materials, and systems (electrical and framing). Want to transform your grease-spotted garage into a functional family room? Or add workshop space, or a craft room? Maybe you don't even have a garage, just a carport that needs enclosing. You'll find out how it's all done (and how to do it yourself, if you like), from finishing a floor to adding a door.

So reclaim and renovate your garage space with the tips and techniques here. (And hey—that coal chute might even be worth something now.).

GARAGE DESIGN

Tired of tripping over boxes and bikes to get to your car? Want a private corner for working on crafts? Need some extra living area that's really livable? For many folks, the garage is the final frontier of unfinished home space, and it can offer unexpected potential for a range of new uses. Whatever your makeover plans, the more you know about garage design and construction, the better able you'll be to turn your dream project into reality.

In this chapter we'll cover broad topics such as garage styles, types, and layouts. Then we'll look closely at fine details like garage and entry door types and placement—even windows, ceilings, and exterior sheathing options. If your makeover plans call for modifying walls, we'll let you know which types of construction lend themselves to this, and which don't.

GARAGE STYLES

Most garages have square or rectangular footprints; the main difference in style concerns how the roof is framed. The four most common roof styles are: gable, reverse gable, hip, and gambrel. Since most garages are sited right next to a house or attached directly to it, it's important that its style matches that of the house.

Gable. The most common garage is the gable style. With this style, the two halves of the roof are symmetrical and join together to form a triangle, as illustrated at right. The garage door is installed in one of the gabled ends. These structures are easy to frame and economical to build. They also provide excellent load-bearing capabilities, as well as good drainage.

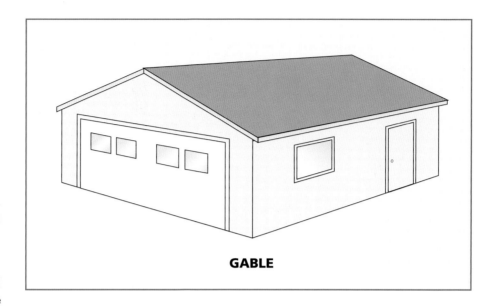

GABLE

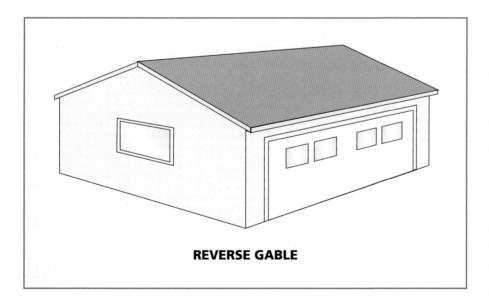

REVERSE GABLE

Reverse gable. A reverse-gable garage is identical to a gable garage with one very important difference: Instead of the door being located in one of the gabled ends, the door is installed under the eaves on one of the long walls, as illustrated at left. The main reason this design is chosen over a gable often concerns how the garage lies in relation to the street. For example, if the gable of the planned garage aligns with the gable on the home, you can run the driveway straight in from the street if you use the reverse-gable design. If you were to choose a standard gable, you'd need to run a driveway around to the gabled end—and that would require a larger lot.

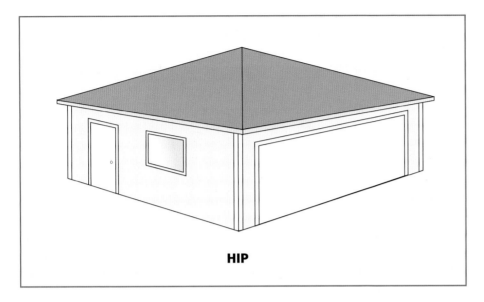

HIP

Hip. On a hip-roof garage, all four gabled sides of the roof lean in toward the center. These ends may run all the way to the center, creating a pyramid-like roof (as illustrated at left), or they may run partially in, leaving a flat portion near the center. In either case, the overhang runs around the entire perimeter and offers the best protection against the elements for you and your garage. The reason they're not more common is that the complex roof line is much more difficult to frame (and therefore more costly).

Gambrel. A gambrel garage is basically a standard gable garage with two pitches on each slope. Varying the pitch like this creates additional headroom and space above the garage, as illustrated at right. This space can be pressed into service as storage, or to provide a work area such as a studio or workshop. The roof framing is more complex, but the additional space often makes it worth the effort.

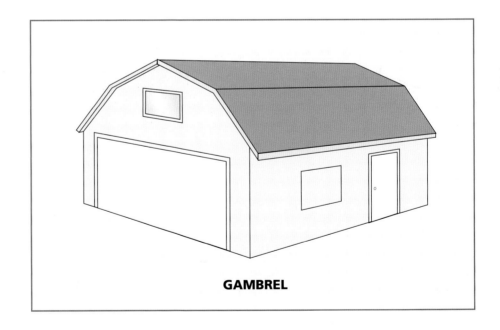

GAMBREL

GARAGE EXTERIORS

■ Although the roof framing is used to identify the style of garage, how the garage exterior is treated will have a great impact on the overall look or impression of the garage. Common themes are Mission, Victorian, Colonial, Tudor, contemporary, and modern.

Mission. The Mission, or Arts & Crafts, style is based on a movement popularized by Gustav Stickley in the United States in the 1890s. The style embraces simplicity and honesty in construction. Bungalow homes in this style are characterized by large overhangs, exposed eaves, roof brackets, and multiple siding materials. Copper light fixtures often adorn the exterior, typically with mica or stained glass to diffuse the light. Notice how the garage doors in the top photo blend in with the wood front door of the home.

Victorian. The Victorian style (often called Queen Anne) is known for its ornamentation and complexity. It originated in Great Britain and became an instant success in America. Irregular-shaped windows, stained glass, complex roofs, and filigree create an interesting exterior. Fanciful scrollwork, delicate spindles, and turned columns, along with varying siding materials, offer plenty of opportunity to spice up the exterior with contrasting colors; this makes the details "pop." Modern versions, like the home shown in the middle photo, often tone down the ornamentation, but still keep architectural details like the tower or "turret" above the porch. The reverse-gable garage presents a clean front that matches the main structure so well it looks like part of the house.

Colonial. Colonial style can be identified by its symmetrical facades, where windows are arranged flanking a central doorway. Half columns typically surround the door as well, and most entryway doors are topped with a fanlight. Sidelights for the entryway door are also common. Windows are usually a combination of 6, 8, 9, or 12 panes of glass in each sash. Notice how well the garage in the bottom photo mimics the style of the house, especially the hip-roof framing.

Tudor. With their roots in 16th-century England, Tudor-style homes often mimic medieval cottages, complete with pseudo-thatched roofs. A Tudor building features lavish use of stone, heavy chimneys, and decorative half-timbering. Tudor structures typically feature steeply pitched roofs with prominent cross gables. The faux half-timbering used these days is strictly decorative, and merely suggests the underlying structural framework. In the top photo, the end of the garage is styled to match the gable above the front entryway.

Contemporary. Strong lines and natural materials (or lookalikes) are the hallmark of the contemporary style. Almost no bold color is used—just calming neutrals that harmonize. This eclectic style frequently combines high-tech surfaces (like the curved glass block in the home in the middle photo) with handmade accessories like lighting or hardware (such as the custom curved rail on the second-floor deck). Although the exterior of the garage in the photo matches the home well enough, the higher-pitched roof detracts from the overall impression. For a true match, a lower-pitched roof would have worked better.

Modern. With a modern home, the emphasis is on architectural shapes and strong lines. Exterior walls are often adorned with geometric patterns, tending toward muted tones; accents can borrow from almost any style. Notice how the column details of the garage shown in the bottom photo match those of the house. Today's new homes typically feature a clean look that never really goes out of style. Another plus is modern style's versatility: Re-paint the walls and change the accent details, and you can have a whole new look.

GARAGE TYPES

■ There are two main criteria used to describe garage type: size and location. Size is usually defined by how many cars the garage can hold (such as a 1-, 2-, or 3-car garage). Location refers to where the garage is in relation to the house: attached or freestanding. An example of garage type is a 2-car attached garage, or a 1-car freestanding garage.

Single. For the most part, you'll find a 1-car garage (like the one shown in the top photo) only with older homes. Occasionally, you may see one on a lot with a newer home as a freestanding unit that serves as a workshop or studio. Slightly larger versions (1½-car garages) provide room for a car plus some storage space; see page 15 for typical garage sizes.

Double. Beginning in the early 1970s, virtually all new homes were built with 2-car garages to suit America's increasing dependence on automobiles. To make the garage even more convenient, most double-car garages were attached directly to the house, as shown in the middle photo. This eliminated the need to walk from the garage to the house and was particularly appreciated in bad weather. Here again, slightly larger versions (2½-car garages) were built to allow for 2 cars plus storage.

Triple. The standard in new homes is rapidly moving toward the 3-car garage, as shown in the bottom photo. Even if the homeowner doesn't have 3 cars, the additional space can be used to store a boat, camper, or other recreational equipment. Alternatively, the extra space can be converted into a craft room, a workshop, or even a game room.

Multi-level. Another increasingly popular garage type is the multi-level garage. This type of garage may offer two different levels of driveway to accommodate tall vehicles (such as a recreational vehicle). A more common version uses a single-level driveway and varying-height doors to accommodate taller vehicles, as with the garage shown in the top photo.

Attached. A garage may be either attached to the house or freestanding. Attached garages, like the one shown in the middle photo, offer people protection from the weather. They also provide better security, since you can drive in, close the door (via a door opener), and then enter the house through the garage. The downside to this type of garage is that it can provide easy access to your home for anyone who can get into the garage. That's why it's important to select a garage door opener that has a complex security code and can also be locked via the remote (for more on choosing garage door openers, see page 42).

Freestanding. A freestanding garage like the one shown in the bottom photo doesn't offer protection from the elements, or the drive-in personal security of an attached garage. It does, though, have a few advantages. First, if part of the garage is used as a workshop, any noise or dust generated in the garage will be self-contained. This is not the case with an attached garage, where noise can easily travel through adjoining walls. Also, if someone breaks into your freestanding garage, they won't have access to your home, as they would with most attached garages.

GARAGE DOOR STYLES

Although there aren't quite as many garage door styles as there are entry door styles, there are still myriad options to choose from. All of the doors shown on these two pages are just a small sample of designs available from a single, major garage door manufacturer, Clopay (www.clopaydoor.com).

Spanish style. The stout wood timbers and decorative black iron hardware of the garage door in the top photo combine to create a look that would work well in a Spanish hacienda, a Mediterranean villa, or a contemporary Santa Fe–style home.

Mission style. Short or long panels plus a wide variety of window and grille options create a look that is as comfortable in a Mission-style garage (like the one shown in the middle photo) as it would be in a Shaker-style garage. The windows can be rectangular, as shown here, or arched (like the Clopay door from their Galley Collection that we used for the carport conversion on pages 64–65).

Colonial style. The stunning custom doors below are a good example of what you can get in a custom door: almost anything you want. Custom grilles create the multipane-look windows. These high arched windows evoke an image of a vintage firehouse that would blend in seamlessly with many Colonial-style homes.

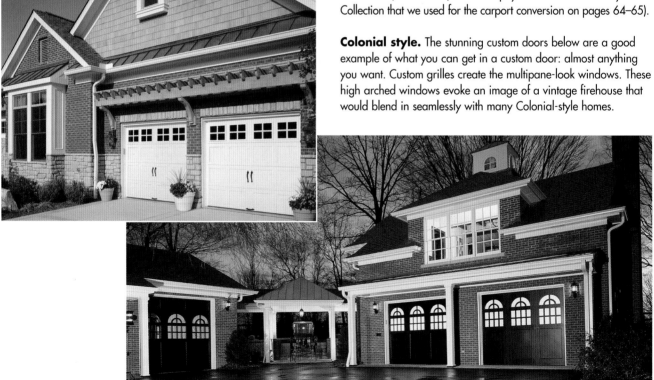

Contemporary style. The innovative design of Clopay's Avante Collection combines sleek, modern lines with high-tech materials. In the garage door shown in the top photo, a pre-painted anodized aluminum frame can hold a variety of materials, including clear glass or acrylic, or frosted, tinted, and even mirrored glass. All of the glass is tempered, and it may be single-pane or insulated.

Traditional style. The wood door shown in the middle photo is from Clopay's custom Reserve Collection. These are available in many species of wood, along with a variety of panel and window configurations, to blend in with almost any look. The door shown here would look at home anywhere from a small farm or ranch to a country estate.

Carriage style. Reminiscent of the doors that adorned carriage houses of yesteryear, the doors shown in the bottom photo offer a classic look but with the strength and durability of steel. This door is from Clopay's Coachman Collection and consists of four layers: steel, insulation, more steel, and a composite overlay to offer a great look that's virtually maintenance-free.

ENTRY DOORS

■ A factor to consider when building or modifying a garage (such as converting a carport to a garage, as described on pages 98–103) is the entry door or doors—the type, style, and location.

Types of entry doors. Entry doors may be single- or double-wide, as shown in the top and middle photos, respectively. Single-wide entry doors are suitable for most garages. It's best to choose one that's at least 36" wide to allow plenty of clearance for moving storage items in and out of the garage. A double-wide door, where both halves open, is well-suited to garages with attached workshops. It's a lot easier to wrestle in a sheet of plywood if the door opening is extra wide. Most double-wide doors start at a width of 4 feet, and go up (or out) in 1-foot increments. Five- and 6-foot-wide double-wide doors are common.

Besides the width of the door, you'll need to decide on a material and style. Metal doors are becoming increasingly popular, as they offer the look of wood but are virtually maintenance-free. Doors with windows let in light, but they also allow a full view of the contents of the garage. For better security, consider ordering a door with frosted glass windows.

Style choices. There are so many style options for entry doors, that odds are you'll be able to find one that blends in well with the rest of your home. In the bottom photo, note how good the garage entry door looks alongside the rest of the home. It's such a good fit that you might think it's the entry for the home instead of the garage.

ENTRY DOOR PLACEMENT

In addition to the type of entry door or doors you choose for your garage, you'll also need to decide where to locate them. The objective here, naturally, is to provide the best access to the garage. Much of this will depend on whether the garage is attached or freestanding, and on the location of the garage door or doors.

The three most common options are illustrated in the drawing at right. You'll find it more convenient to have multiple entry doors, if possible. For example, if you combine options 1 and 3 in the drawing, you can enter the garage (without opening the garage door), pick something up, and pass directly out into the backyard.

As you narrow your choices for locating the entry door, keep in mind a couple of items. First, think about access and traffic flow in all four seasons. What might seem like an ideal spot in the summer could turn out to be inaccessible in the winter. It's also a good idea to mentally walk around the garage and observe how the entry door or doors will be viewed from the house and the street.

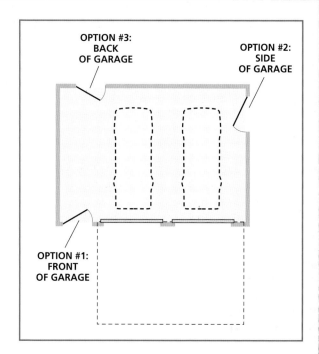

OPTION #3:
BACK
OF GARAGE

OPTION #2:
SIDE
OF GARAGE

OPTION #1:
FRONT
OF GARAGE

WINDOWS

■ If you've flipped through home magazines or strolled the home center aisles, you have an idea of the array of window styles, finishes, and formats available today—and that's just the stock items. Add in custom-order solutions to solve a problem or match a theme, and it opens up a new level of makeover possibilities. In addition to standard windows, you can bring light into your garage with skylights or Solatubes.

Double-hung. The most common style of window installed in garages is the double-hung variety, like the window in the top photo. This is often done simply to match the windows in the home (for more on the various types of windows, see pages 38–39). Most windows made today are clad; that is, a wood core is wrapped or "clad" with vinyl or metal, like the unit shown in the inset photo. This combination provides the strength and mass of wood with the maintenance-free features of metal or wood. Note: Instead of clear glass, consider going with frosted glass; it offers additional privacy while still letting in light.

Skylights. Skylights, like the one shown in the middle photo, are a great way to get a lot of light into your garage. Since these units require cutting a hole in your roof and some reframing (unless the skylights you're using are the slim variety designed to fit between ceiling joists), it's best to have this done prior to installing shingles. If there's a new roof in your garage's future, the best time to install a skylight is after the old shingling is torn off and before the new shingles are installed.

Solatubes. We all know that natural light is the best for most rooms. The problem is, we don't always have the correct size, number, or placement of windows we'd like. The solution? Bring light in through the ceiling. That's exactly what Solatubes tubular skylights are designed to do—they capture sunlight on the roof and redirect it down through a highly reflective tube, through a diffuser, and into your room. The only downside to one of these is that it requires cutting a hole in your roof. If you're not comfortable doing that, consider hiring a roofing contractor to install the unit.

Armed with modest carpentry skills, the average homeowner can install one of these units in an afternoon. The only problem will be that as soon as you're done, you're going to want to install more. Complete installation instructions can be found at Solatube's website (www.solatube.com).

GARAGE WALLS

■ The walls of most garages are constructed of one of three materials: dimension lumber, concrete blocks, or bricks. Which material was originally used to construct your garage will have a great impact on how easy or difficult it is to remodel or make over your garage. Besides brick and block, your exterior options include T1-11, stone, siding, or stucco; see page 22 for more on these materials.

Dimension lumber. A garage made with dimension lumber, commonly referred to as being "stick-built," is the easiest to work with for remodeling. In most garages, the walls attach directly to the concrete slab via J-bolts, as illustrated in the example on the left in the bottom drawing. The transition piece from slab to wall is usually pressure-treated wood and is commonly called a mudsill. Wall studs are spaced 16" on center, and the strength of the wall comes from the exterior sheeting that ties all the individual framing members together. The interior walls may or may not be covered.

Concrete block. When walls are made of concrete block, they're stout but hard to work with. Blocks are stacked on top of each other directly on a concrete slab or footing, as illustrated in the middle example in the bottom drawing. Mortar is sandwiched between the blocks to hold them together. Since these walls are effectively solid, it's difficult and time-consuming to modify them. If your makeover plans call for modifying a concrete block wall, consider hiring a licensed concrete contractor.

Brick. When many people see a brick house or garage, they assume the walls are made of stacked brick. Although this is possible in some cases, most brick structures are actually stick-framed and have a brick-veneered exterior. Notice the similarity between the left and right examples in the bottom drawing. The big difference between the stick-framed and "brick" wall is the exterior covering. With the stick-built, it's siding; on the brick wall, it's a layer of bricks held in place with a ledge strip and fasteners driven into the wall studs. These fasteners are driven in between bricks and then covered with mortar. When dry, the mortar grips the fastener, which is secured to the studs to fully support the bricks. Unless your makeover plans call for modifying the exterior of the garage, you'll find that a "brick" wall is as easy to work with as a stick-built wall since it's also really a stick-built wall.

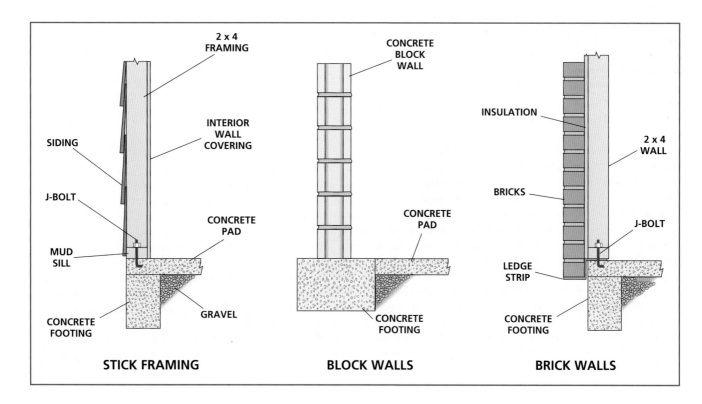

T1-11. Softwood plywood siding is available with a wide range of surface treatments, such as V-grooves or channel grooves, and with brushed or rough-sawn textures. The most common of these that's frequently used for exterior sheathing (as shown in the top photo) is called T1-11; it's sold at most home centers. In addition to working well as exterior sheathing, T1-11 is also great for covering the interior walls of a garage (as described on page 119). Sure, it's more expensive than drywall; but it looks great, and because it's plywood, you can screw into it anywhere. This makes it ideal in a shop, where you have a lot of "stuff" hanging off the walls.

Stone. For the most part, stone exteriors like the one shown in the middle photo are actually just a stone veneer applied to exterior sheathing. These exteriors are mostly maintenance-free and can be applied to any structure. The stone in the photo is made by Eldorado Stone (www.eldoradostone.com).

Siding. If your garage was built within the last 15 years and has siding, chances are that it's hardboard. Hardboard (commonly referred to as Masonite, the brand name of a leading manufacturer) is an engineered product that is hard, dense, and relatively flat. Hardboard siding is a mixture of finely ground processed wood and resins which are bonded together under heat and pressure. The exterior surface is typically molded to resemble wood grain. Most hardboard siding is either primed or fully painted and comes ready to install.

Because it's still wood, hardboard siding requires frequent re-painting. You can avoid this by choosing metal or vinyl siding, both of which are mostly maintenance-free (as shown in the bottom left photo). The downside to metal siding is that it dents easily. Vinyl siding doesn't dent so easily, but can't be painted, so you have to stick with the color selection provided by the manufacturer.

Stucco. Stucco has always been a fairly hardy exterior. It's basically a mortar that's applied to exterior walls (bottom right photo). To provide something for the stucco to grip, the exterior walls are first covered with wire mesh. Stucco can be painted and can be touched up as needed. Its main downside: a fairly well-deserved reputation for being tough to repair. If your garage makeover calls for modifying stucco walls, consider calling in a pro.

CEILING OPTIONS

■ The type of ceiling you choose to make over your garage will depend mostly on how you'll use the new space. If your main use is storage, drywall will do. For use as a living space, you may want to install ceiling paneling. If the space will be used as a workshop or family room, consider noise-dampening acoustical tile.

Drywall. Drywall is the least expensive ceiling material to install. It also goes up relatively fast (see pages 122–125) and can be painted to match the décor. Many design pros will tell you that the only color for a ceiling is white, because it tends to draw the eyes up and help make the room seem larger (top left photo). But it's also true that you can change a room's appearance for the better with a little color. Subtle pastels like light yellow and pale green can soften the feel of a room to create a more inviting or calmer environment. Alternatively, you can make a bold statement with color.

Ceiling paneling. Ceiling paneling (top right photo) has recently become popular, thanks to some of the new installation methods that manufacturers have designed. With a snap-in-place system, the panels go up in an afternoon. The only challenge is getting the grid system in place so the tracks are parallel and equally spaced. This is not a problem if you have patience and take your time. Most ceiling paneling is covered with laminate, so it doesn't require any special care. This is basically the same material used for laminate flooring, but thinner. These panels are a great choice for adding flair to a room, whether they're colored a warm wood tone, a whitewashed effect, or something in between.

Acoustical tile. Acoustical tile goes up much like ceiling paneling and also does a great job of concealing a bad ceiling. Acoustical tile comes in many patterns and almost always in white. It is available in 12"-square tiles (middle photo) that can be fastened to furring strips attached to ceiling joists. Alternatively, if you have plenty of ceiling height, you can purchase larger tiles (2' square or 2'×4') and drop these into a grid suspended from the ceiling, as shown in the bottom photo. Installing the grid for a suspended ceiling can take quite a bit of time, as it's often a challenge to get all the grid parts leveled.

STORAGE

▦ Since so many homeowners utilize their garages as primary or secondary storage spaces, it's no wonder there are so many different types of storage systems made specifically for the garage. The two most popular types of storage products are full-wall systems and specialty hangers.

Systems. There are numerous full-wall storage systems available to meet your storage needs. Some use a special wall covering that's made to accept a wide variety of holders, like the Grid Iron system shown in the top photo (www.gridironusa.com). With this system you attach heavy-duty metal panels to your wall. The built-in lips on the panel accept sturdy holders for shelves and other equipment. Other versions include extruded plastic wall panels or "track" systems that attach to the wall and accept various holders (see pages 44–45 for more on storage systems).

Specialty hangers. If you don't want a full-wall system, there are a couple of manufacturers that make stand-alone specialty hangers like the Racor (www.racorinc.com) units shown in the bottom photo. Most of these attach to a special "wall dock" that makes installing or moving the hanger a snap. These hangers are designed to hold everything from fishing rods and mountain bikes to power tools and shop supplies.

Shop-built. Although manufactured systems are great, their one drawback is cost. You can easily spend $1,000 or more for a full-wall system. If you like the idea of a wall system but not the cost, consider building our easy-to-make wall storage system shown in the middle photo. (Full details and instructions for this system are on pages 172–175.)

GARAGE DRIVEWAYS

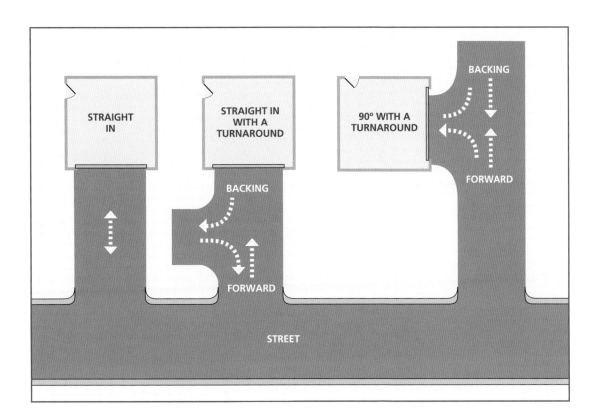

STRAIGHT
IN

STRAIGHT IN
WITH A
TURNAROUND

90° WITH A
TURNAROUND

BACKING

FORWARD

BACKING

FORWARD

STREET

A garage makeover may involve changing the location of the garage door. If this is in your plans, you'll probably also need to modify the driveway. The three most common ways a garage connects to the street are: straight in, straight in with a turnaround, and 90 degrees with a turnaround, as illustrated in the drawing above.

In most cases, short driveways are sized to match the width of the garage. Longer driveways, on the other hand, are usually only single-car in width, to hold down costs. They may or may not include a turnaround area as shown.

Before you modify a garage, you should know that in many areas, zoning restrictions and local building codes may regulate what you can legally do to your garage, as well as defining its maximum dimensions. Might there be restrictions on your structure? That depends on your town, and the type and size of your structure. The only way to find out is to consult your local building inspector. The inspector willl be able to tell you whether any restrictions apply and will also advise whether you'll need a building permit, and an inspection to make sure that the structure meets minimum code requirements.

CHOOSING MATERIALS

L ike any makeover, revamping a garage requires lots of decisions about which materials to use for your projects. Naturally, you want to spend your makeover dollars wisely and get the most for your money. But buying the costliest product you can afford may not always be the best choice. Quite often, a less expensive choice will do the job just as well. That's why you need to know as much as possible about each material you select.

This chapter will first take you through the many options involved in a garage makeover: flooring, framing, sheathing, insulation, wall coverings, windows, entry doors, garage doors, and garage door openers. Then, you'll find detailed info on cabinets, storage systems, lighting, and even driveway paving choices—everything you'll need for a successful makeover.

2

FLOORING, *continued*

Epoxy coating. Epoxy coatings like the Rust-Oleum EpoxyShield system used to seal the floor shown in the top photo have become an increasingly popular choice for garage makeovers. Epoxy coatings protect against gasoline, antifreeze, motor oil, salt, and hot tire pick-up. They are easy to apply and easy to maintain. Most systems come as kits that include everything you need for the project. There are both water-based and solvent-based systems; we recommend the water-based systems, as they offer low odor and easy cleanup. Note: To get a strong bond between the epoxy coating and the concrete, it's imperative that you follow the manufacturer's cleaning instructions to the letter (see pages 88–90 for more on applying an epoxy coating).

Concrete paint. Another way to seal concrete and keep out dirt and debris is to paint it. Most paint manufacturers sell paint designed specifically for covering concrete, as shown in the middle inset photo. Because the paint bonds to the concrete itself, it's critical that the concrete be super-clean and completely dry before paint is applied. See pages 80–82 for more on cleaning, patching, and painting concrete.

Concrete stains. Most homeowners don't realize that you can stain concrete, but you can, and it's easy. Stains are an excellent way to give color to concrete without worrying about the regular maintenance that paint usually requires. Most stains are semi-transparent, so you'll still be able to see that the underlying surface is concrete, as shown in the inset photo at right. These stains are easy to apply with a roller, and you can refresh them as needed by first cleaning the concrete and then applying a fresh coat of stain.

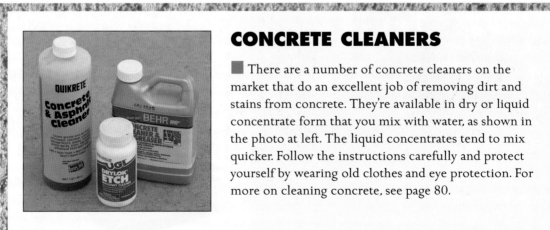

CONCRETE CLEANERS

There are a number of concrete cleaners on the market that do an excellent job of removing dirt and stains from concrete. They're available in dry or liquid concentrate form that you mix with water, as shown in the photo at left. The liquid concentrates tend to mix quicker. Follow the instructions carefully and protect yourself by wearing old clothes and eye protection. For more on cleaning concrete, see page 80.

ROLL-OUT FLOORING

■ Coatings, such as epoxy and paint, do a good job of sealing and protecting concrete, but they don't offer any cushioning, or anti-fatigue properties. And if you want to hose off a coated floor, you have to be careful to keep water and cleaners off your garage walls. There is a flooring option that not only solves these problems, but also looks great: roll-out flooring. The roll-out flooring shown here, called G-Floor, is manufactured by Better Life Technology, LLC (www.bltllc.com) and is 100% high-quality polyvinyl, through and through. The 50- to 80-mm-thick pad helps reduce fatigue, protects your concrete floor, and serves as a vapor barrier.

G-Floor is available in these standard sizes: 7.5' wide × 14', 17', or 20' long; 8' wide × 22' long; 9' wide × 20' long; and 10' wide × 22' long. Parking pads are also available in a variety of sizes and in six colors: midnight black, sandstone, racing blue, forest green, slate grey, and brick red. BLT offers three flooring patterns: diamond tread pattern, coin pattern, and rib pattern; see below.

Because G-Floor requires no adhesives—you basically just roll it out onto your floor (see pages 94–95)—it's a snap to install. But what we really like about it is that when it gets dirty, you just pull it out onto your driveway and spray it down, as shown in the top photo. Your floor gets clean without water damage to your garage walls.

Diamond tread pattern: Offered in specially formulated, heavy-duty, commercial- and industrial-grade material.

Coin pattern: Reduces the amount of dirt tracked into the home.

Ribbed pattern: Controls debris and channels liquids away.

WALL FRAMING

■ The walls in most garages are "stick-built." That is, they're constructed of dimension lumber. Although dimension lumber is manufactured in 1-foot increments, 2-foot increments are more common. The width of softwood lumber varies from 2" to 16", usually in 2" increments; dimension lumber ranges in thickness from 2" to 5".

Grades. When dimension lumber is graded or sorted by its characteristics, much more than appearance comes into play—strength, stiffness, and other mechanical properties are all taken into consideration; see the chart below. There are four grades of structural light framing lumber: Select structural, No. 1, No. 2, and No. 3. Select structural is the highest grade in structural light framing and is recommended where appearance is as important as strength and stiffness. When appearance is still important but is secondary to strength, No. 1 grade is the best choice. No. 2 structural light framing lumber is recommended for general construction; when strength is not a factor, No. 3 grade can be used.

Header spans. Anytime there's an opening in a wall and studs have to be removed, a header is installed to assume the load of the removed stud or studs. The size of the header you will use will depend on the distance it has to span. As a general rule of thumb, the longer the span, the stouter the header; see the chart below.

RECOMMENDED SPANS FOR HEADERS

Size	Grade (Douglas fir)	Maximum Span (in feet)
4×4	#2	4
4×6	#2	6
4×8	#2	8
4×10	#2	10
4×12	#2	12
4×14	#1	16

SOFTWOOD GRADES FOR DIMENSION LUMBER

Classification	Grade	Application
Structural light framing	SEL STR	Used when good appearance is required along with strength and stiffness
	No. 1	Recommended where good appearance is desired but is secondary to strength and stiffness
	No. 2	Used in general construction
	No. 3	Appropriate for general construction where strength is generally not a factor
Structural joists and planks	CONST	General framing applications; graded for strength and serviceability
	STAND	Used for general framing, often along with CONST lumber
	UTIL	Recommended where economies are desired for studs, blocking, plates, and bracing
	STUD	A separate grade that identifies pieces suitable for all stud uses, including load-bearing walls; restrictions on crook, wane, and edge knots make this popular for wall construction
	Economy	This grade is available in all four of the above categories—not intended for structural applications

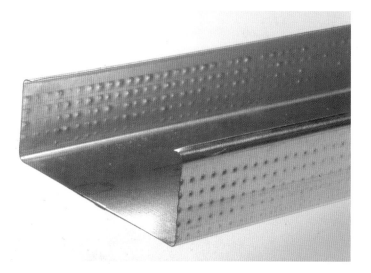

Metal framing. Steel studs are becoming increasingly popular as a replacement for wood studs. They're easy to use, are perfectly straight, and cost about the same as a wood stud. Steel studs are available in two common grades or categories: load-bearing (LB) and non-load-bearing (NLB). NLB drywall studs are typically made of 25-gauge steel and should be used only for partition walls; LB studs use a heavier gauge to handle the additional stress; see below.

Load-bearing studs can usually be identified by the bent lip at the edge of the flange, as shown in the top photo. This added lip helps keep the stud rigid so that it can support heavier loads. Most manufacturers of LB studs also make track without lips so that the studs can slip in place without the need of any cutting. These tracks are the equivalent of top and sole plates. Studs and tracks are available in widths ranging from 1⅝" to 6".

KNOCKOUTS AND GROMMETS

■ Most brands of metal framing offer pre-punched knockouts for running electrical lines, as shown in the middle photo. Because the edges of the knockouts are razor-sharp, the framing manufacturers sell plastic grommets (bushings) that easily snap into place to protect the wiring, as shown in the bottom photo. Insert a bushing into each side of the metal stud and press the pieces together until they snap together. Note: If you're planning on using these cutouts to run wiring, take care as you cut the studs to length (and position them) so that the cutouts line up horizontally. This will simplify pulling the cable through the studs.

INTERIOR SHEATHING

There are several types of interior sheathing to choose from to cover the interior walls of your garage: drywall, T1-11, plywood, plastic storage panels, and pegboard. You can also mix and match materials to meet your needs.

Drywall. Many garage makeover projects require removing old walls and/or installing new walls—and this means new sheathing. The easiest interior wall sheathing to install is drywall. We recommend $1/2$" drywall whenever possible, since it holds up better over time than thinner drywall (top photo). When installing drywall in rooms where moisture is present, make sure to use moisture-resistant drywall. This is easy to distinguish from standard drywall by its green color.

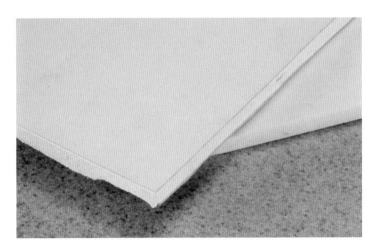

T1-11. Plywood known as T1-11 is a composite plywood panel that comes in 4-foot-wide sheets manufactured in 8-, 9-, and 10-foot lengths (middle photo). Panels range in thickness from $3/8$" to $5/8$"; however, most panels are $7/16$". Panels have either smooth, stucco, or wood-grain embossed surfaces. Some wood-grain panels have vertical grooves spaced every 4" to 8". Although T1-11 is sold as exterior siding, it works great as interior sheathing for workshop space in a garage. Besides being hard to ding and dent, T1-11 also offers optimum flexibility for hanging items on the wall. The multi-ply construction provides excellent purchase for fasteners anywhere on a panel— you don't have to hunt for a stud to mount most light to medium-heavy objects.

Plywood. Most softwood plywood is manufactured for use in either industrial or construction applications. That's why most standards for softwood plywood deal exclusively with how it must perform in a designated application, rather than its appearance. Like T1-11 (see above), softwood plywood offers unlimited flexibility for mounting objects on the wall (bottom photo). If moisture is a concern in your garage, make sure to choose an outdoor-rated plywood. There are three exposure durability classifications for plywood: Exterior, Exposure 1, and Exposure 2. Exterior panels have a fully waterproofed bond and are designed for applications subject to permanent exposure to moisture. Exposure 1 panels should be used for protected applications where the glue bond must be waterproof. Exposure 2 panels are intended for protected construction and industrial applications.

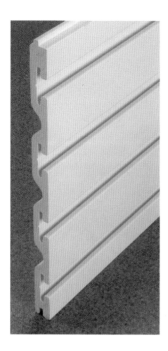

Plastic or vinyl storage panels. Want an easy way to add an instant storage surface to a wall, or a section of wall? You can't go wrong with panels like the GearWall panels shown in the top left photo, manufactured by Gladiator GarageWorks (www.gladiatorgw.com). Not only are these panels a snap to install, they're also a great way to get things organized. GearWall panels are a heavy-duty, patent-pending slot-wall system that comes in 1-foot by 8-foot units. The panels easily attach to wood studs or to drywall over wood studs. All Gladiator wall accessories and wall GearBoxes can be used with these panels.

Pegboard. Pegboard has been a standard in garages for decades. This popular, 1/4" perforated hardboard product accepts a wide variety of pegboard hooks and holders. DPI, Inc., manufactures a line of metallic pegboard that's especially well suited for garage interiors (www.decpanels.com), as shown in the top right photo. These metallic panels are finished with an acrylic polymer topcoat to give them a long-lasting, attractive finish. The result is a tough, versatile wall panel perfect for commercial or residential use.

A SCREENED WALL

Instead of interior sheathing, how about a nice screened wall to let in cool breezes in the summer, while keeping out annoying insects? Sounds good, but what about the winter? The solution is simple— open up your garage door and screen the opening. This may sound impractical at first, but not if you use a retractable screen manufactured by Fly Away AgriProducts (www.flyawayagri.com). Fly Away makes three versions of their retractable screen; see below. Any of these can be custom-built to fit any size opening.

Automatic screen: The ultimate in retractable screens is a fully automated unit. Just push a button to raise or lower the screen.

Hand-crank screen: A less-expensive version of the fully automatic screen is one that's raised and lowered via an easy-to-use hand crank.

Snap-on screen: Flyaway even makes an economy screen that snaps in place, much like a topper for a pickup truck. Although it takes a bit to install or remove the screen, it's economical.

INSULATION

If you're converting a carport into a garage or converting your garage to living space, you'll probably want to insulate the walls and ceiling to keep the space warm in the winter and cool in the summer. The three most common types of insulation you'll choose from are: rigid insulation, fiberglass, and blown-in cellulose.

Rigid insulation. Rigid insulation or foamboard (top photo) is often used to increase the thermal performance of a wall. It can be applied directly over sheathing before siding is installed; or, it may be installed to the inside of a wall. Rigid foam is commonly available in thicknesses ranging from 1/2" to 2", and comes in 4×8-foot sheets or trimmed into panels designed to fit common stud spacing patterns. When applied to an interior wall, foamboard is often glued in place with construction adhesive.

Fiberglass. Fiberglass insulation has long been the favorite in construction. It cuts easily, goes up quickly, and has admirable insulation properties. Fiberglass insulation comes in faced or unfaced rolls or pre-cut lengths (bottom left photo). The facing

is either paper or a vapor retarder—both versions have tabs that are folded over the studs and stapled in place. When unfaced batts are installed in walls, a continuous vapor retarder should be used to cover the studs and insulation—this system actually provides a better barrier than faced insulation, since the barrier is continuous.

Ceiling insulation. There are numerous products available for insulating a ceiling. Fiberglass ceiling batts can be faced or unfaced, and are typically pre-cut to fit between rafters. They can be placed directly on top of the existing ceiling or on top of ceiling panels, as shown in the bottom right photo. Acoustical ceiling tiles also offer some insulating properties in addition to their sound-dampening ability. Cellulose insulation is popular since it can be blown in to fill the spaces between rafters. Most home centers that sell cellulose also rent the blower for a nominal charge. Both fiberglass and cellulose do a good job of insulating, but fiberglass batts are much more remodel-friendly (just imagine cutting a hole in the ceiling at some future date and having loose cellulose come pouring out).

DECORATIVE WALL COVERINGS

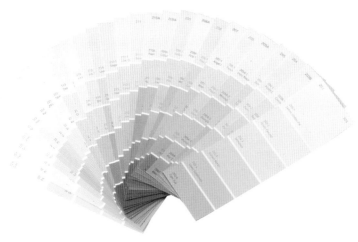

■ If you're converting your garage into a living space, you'll probably want to apply a decorative wall covering such as paint, wallpaper, or paneling.

Paint. Paint is the easiest, fastest way to make over walls. You'll find every imaginable color available (top photo). For living spaces, a flat latex finish is usually best (try eggshell in kids' areas). Some specialty paints provide texture such as suede, and faux finishes like ragging or sponging help bring a richer, more interesting texture to any painted surface.

Wallpaper. Wallpaper is a bit more challenging to use than paint, but it offers the advantage of thousands of patterns, textures, and shades; you'll find stacks of wallpaper sample books at home and decorating centers (middle photo). Want your walls to look like bamboo, woven cloth, or even metal? Paper is the way to go—but be sure to choose the strippable kind. It's much easier to remove when it's time for another fresh look.

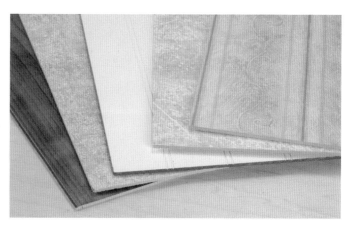

Paneling. Paneling—often called wallboard—is a beautiful, durable, and cost-effective option for wall coverings. It's easy to install, and some types are even moisture-resistant. What's best is that once installed, it's virtually maintenance-free. The paneling shown in the bottom photo is manufactured by DPI (www.decpanels.com). We used a metallic version of pegboard from DPI on our Mechanic's Dream makeover described on pages 66–67.

WINDOWS

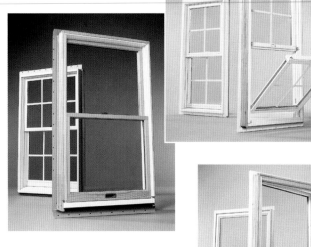

Whether you're converting a carport to a garage, converting a garage to a living space, or just want to bring in more light, you'll need to select from the range of window types and styles available. While styles vary widely, there are five main types of window that lend themselves to a garage makeover: single- and double-hung; casement; awning; sliding; and glass/acrylic block. You'll also need to choose from a number of glazing options; see the sidebar below.

Single- and double-hung. The difference between a single- and a double-hung window is the ability of the upper sash to move. On a single-hung window it's fixed; with a double-hung, it can be raised or lowered (top left photo). The lower sash on both types is movable. When shopping for single- or double-hung windows, look for the tilting-sash variety (top inset photo), as these tilt out for easy cleaning.

Casement. A casement window is any window where the sash is hinged on the side to allow it to pivot in and out like a door (middle photo). Most casement windows project outward and therefore provide significantly better ventilation than sliding windows of equal size. Another reason that a casement window offers better ventilation than a sliding window is that virtually the entire window area can be opened. On sliding windows, only one-half of the available window space can be opened.

GLAZING OPTIONS

The type and number of panes (or glazing) that a window has will greatly affect its insulating properties.

Single pane: The least energy-efficient window is the single-pane variety. Common in older homes, this type of window is suitable only in mild climates. One option that can help with a single-pane window is to have a low-E coating applied to the pane. This coating filters out ultraviolet rays to protect furnishings, while also helping to insulate the home in winter and summer.

Double pane: A double-pane window has two panes of glass separated by an air space. When sealed properly, this air space provides insulation from both summer heat and winter cold. To further increase the insulating properties of the window, some manufacturers inject a safe, colorless gas (such as argon) into this space. A quality gas-filled double-pane window with low-E coatings typically provides an R-value of around 4 to 5. (R-value is the capacity of a material to impede heat flow; the higher the number, the greater the capacity.)

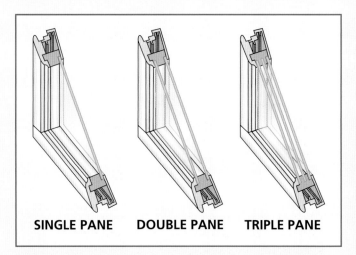

SINGLE PANE   **DOUBLE PANE**   **TRIPLE PANE**

Triple pane: The ultimate in insulated windows is the triple pane. Three panes of glass offer two separate insulating spaces. Here again, these spaces can be filled with argon or another gas to increase the insulating properties. R-values around 10 are common with triple-pane windows. A side benefit of both double- and triple-pane windows is that they also significantly reduce noise transmission. The drawback to both of these is that they're more expensive than single-pane windows.

Awning. Awning windows are hinged at the top and swing open at the bottom, as shown in the top photo. Just like casement windows, awning windows provide greater ventilation than sliding windows (see below), since practically the entire window area can be opened to catch a breeze. Awning windows can be installed so the sash opens outward (such as in a garage or workshop), or inward in the case of a basement window.

Sliding. The big advantage that sliding windows have to offer is cost: they're inexpensive. That's because there are many fewer moving parts in a sliding window than in a casement or double-hung window. On most sliding windows, one half of the window is fixed and the other half slides back and forth in a track (middle photo). Also, since gravity doesn't work against the sliding motion (as it does in a double-hung window), sliding windows tend to be relatively maintenance-free when installed properly.

Glass or plastic block. For light, privacy, and energy efficiency, block windows of glass or lightweight acrylic make sense, especially in an exterior wall. First, they let in more natural light, making interior spaces seem more spacious. At the same time, they protect privacy by partially obscuring the view: Motion can be seen, but not detail. Finally, they insulate against outdoor conditions to help regulate temperature and energy use. The window shown in the bottom photo is acrylic block, which is lighter than traditional glass block and can be retrofit to replace existing windows. The unit shown here is from Hy-Lite Productions, Inc. (www.hylite.com).

GARAGE DOOR MATERIALS

When it comes to shopping for a garage door, you've got a lot of decisions to make. Most homeowners start with appearance (pages 16–17) and then choose among materials (see below) and opening options (see page 41). Material options include wood, metal, glass, or a combination of these. Some garage door manufacturers (like Clopay: www.clopaydoor.com) make metal doors that are almost indistinguishable from wood doors.

Wood. A solid-wood door has a number of advantages over its high-tech cousins. Since it is wood, it can be stained to create a wide variety of custom finishes. And unlike metal and glass doors that are mostly mass-produced, wood doors can be easily altered to fit any opening. This is the type of door to turn to when you've got an odd-shaped or non-standard door opening and you don't want to alter the opening to fit a standard door. On the downside, wood doors are expensive and can be quite heavy. They also require regular maintenance of the finish, since wood tends to deteriorate when exposed to the elements.

Metal. Metal doors can offer the look and feel of wood, but with the strength and durability of steel. Most metal doors, like the Clopay unit shown in the middle photo, are constructed from a number of layers. Clopay uses four layers: a layer of insulation sandwiched between two layers of metal, and an exterior composite overlay to provide a natural wood-grain texture. Common door thicknesses are $1^3/8$" and 2". The R-value of their $1^3/8$" door is 6.5, and the 2"-thick door has a 9.0 R-value. Window and grille options are many, so you can custom-order the look you want.

Glass. Looking for something different in a garage door material? How about glass? Clopay's Avante line of doors utilizes a $2^1/8$"-wide aluminum frame to hold glass panels, as shown in the bottom photo. The glass can be clear, frosted, or mirrored. The frame itself is anodized aluminum that comes in standard white or brown.

DOOR-OPENING OPTIONS

■ So you've decided how you want your new garage door to look and have pretty much settled on the material. Now—how do you want it to open? There are three common opening methods to choose from: sectional, swing-up, and roll-up.

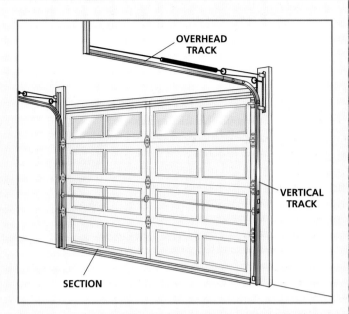

OVERHEAD TRACK

VERTICAL TRACK

SECTION

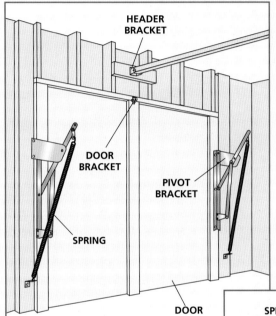

HEADER BRACKET

DOOR BRACKET

PIVOT BRACKET

SPRING

DOOR

Swing-up: Common in older homes, a swing-up door employs a pair of pivot brackets and springs to swing the door up and out of the way, as illustrated in the top left drawing. The door may or may not have a track to help guide the door as it swings up. If you choose a one-piece door, this is your best opening option. The other option—a sliding door setup (similar to a barn door and not shown here)—does not provide the look most homeowners are after for their garage.

Sectional: Sectional garage doors are by far the most common. The door itself is made up of three to five sections, as illustrated in the top right drawing. Rollers attached to the inside face of the door's edge fit into a curved track mounted to the wall and ceiling. A pair of springs or a torsion spring provides the muscle needed to lift the heavy door. In many cases, this will be the opening option you'll want to pick.

Roll-up: Roll-up doors like the one illustrated in the bottom drawing are used primarily in commercial buildings. These industrial-looking doors consist of a rolled steel curtain that is raised and lowered via a spring counterbalance on top of the door. The door may be opened automatically by an opener, or operated manually by way of a loop chain.

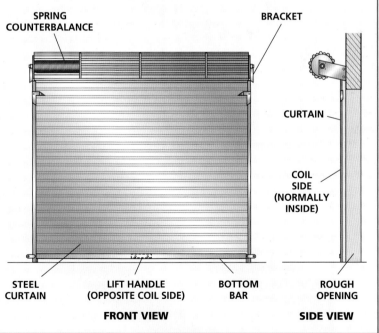

SPRING COUNTERBALANCE

BRACKET

CURTAIN

COIL SIDE (NORMALLY INSIDE)

STEEL CURTAIN

LIFT HANDLE (OPPOSITE COIL SIDE)

BOTTOM BAR

ROUGH OPENING

FRONT VIEW

SIDE VIEW

STORAGE SYSTEMS

■ These days, there's real choice and convenience when you're in the market for storage systems for a garage. Several firms now offer systems designed specifically with the garage (and related spaces) in mind. These include systems manufactured by Rubbermaid, storeWALL, Racor, and Grid Iron.

Rubbermaid. Rubbermaid's storage system is called FastTrack (www.rubbermaid.com). The system consists of rails, cabinets, and accessories that are integrated to create a coordinated, finished look, as shown in the bottom photo. The heart of the system is the very durable FastTrack Rails that attach to your wall studs and can support up to

2,000 pounds each. The FastTrack Rails accept numerous specialty holders that support everything from a wheelbarrow and bikes to power tools, ladders, sports equipment, and hoses. Also available: shelving units, mesh bins and baskets, and multi-purpose hooks. Each holder snaps onto the FastTrack Rail, as shown in the left inset photo, and can be easily unhooked and reconfigured. For a more permanent installation, each holder can be screwed in place.

StoreWALL. StoreWALL takes a different approach with their storage system. Instead of a set of rails, their system uses storeWALL Heavy-Duty panels (www.storewall.com) that are available in five colors, all with a matte finish, as shown in the top photo. The panels can be installed with their hidden fastener system for a super-clean look. Alternatively, the panels can be screwed directly to wall studs or to drywall-covered studs. The panels are made from PVC and come in a variety of widths and lengths. Grooves in the panels accept a variety of accessories (including cabinets) such as those sold by The Accessories Group (www.theaccessoriesgroup.com). Because the grooved panels cover the entire wall, your storage options are extremely flexible.

Racor. Another approach to garage storage is to build individual holders for specific items or groups of items (such as sports gear or power tools). That's what Racor, Inc., has done with their InterChange product line (www.racorinc.com), as shown in the top photo. They created their storage system to meet homeowners' needs for easy installation, storage flexibility, and seasonal access. InterChange provides unlimited modular possibilities for keeping tools, recreation gear, and anything else right where you need it. The beauty of this system is that as you accumulate more "stuff," it's a simple matter to reorganize and add racks. This is all possible because of their innovative two-part WallDocks fasteners. All racks fit on the WallDocks, so you can move or add racks anytime.

Grid Iron. The folks at Grid Iron (www.gidironusa.com) developed a storage system that was inspired by their parent company, which built extremely sturdy merchandise organizers for the retail market. Grid Iron's system is based on unique steel slot-wall panels that feature 1" rolled-steel channels. These channels accept a variety of accessories to make customizing a snap, as shown in the middle photo. This storage system was by far the most heavy-duty that we used for our makeovers. Although you might think we used Grid Iron in a workshop, it's so good-looking that we used it in our living space makeover, shown on pages 72–73. Grid Iron sells startup kits that make ordering what you need simple. We found their ingenious, cantilevered shelving system to be both attractive and sturdy.

ACTIVITY RACKS

Most of the storage system manufacturers have developed specially themed racks designed around a particular activity. Some of the most popular of these are racks for storing sports equipment, like those shown in the bottom photo. Depending on the manufacturer, you can find racks that hold balls of all shapes and sizes, golf equipment, fishing gear, etc. Also popular are specialty racks for holding power tools and other workshop gear.

LIGHTING

In most garages, general lighting comes from a single overhead fixture, either incandescent or fluorescent. Task lighting—lighting designed to illuminate a specific area—is usually under-cabinet lights in the form of strips or "pucks." Accent lighting can be anything from interior cabinet lights to pendants to wall sconces.

Surface-mount. A surface-mount light is any light fixture that attaches directly to the ceiling, like the hanging lamp shown in the top left photo. Pendant lights are perfect for lighting living spaces. There are two basic versions of a pendant light: one where the light is suspended simply by its electrical cord, and one like that shown here, where the light is suspended via a metal rod or chain that hides the electrical cord.

Recessed. The body of a recessed light is set into the ceiling so all you see is the trim, as shown in the top right photo. Some recessed lights attach to the ceiling with a set of clips; others attach directly to ceiling joists or electrical boxes attached to them. Alternatively, the light can attach to a pair of sliding brackets that are fastened to the ceiling joists. When selecting recessed cans, make sure to choose the type that's rated for insulation contact. These lights can be installed in the ceiling without having to move the insulation out of the way (which would create an unwanted path for warm air to leak out of your garage). For the ultimate in flexibility, choose cans that have pivoting lenses so you can direct the light where you need it most.

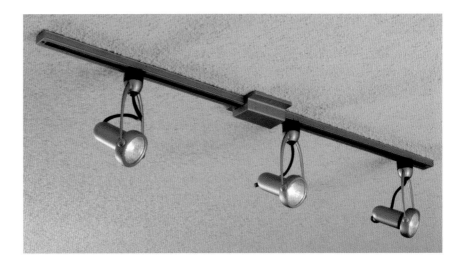

Track. Track lighting is a special type of surface-mount light and is a great way to provide customizable lighting in your garage; individual lamps snap into a track anywhere along its length (as shown in the bottom photo) to spotlight different areas of the room or special wall treatments. You can either replace an existing fixture with track lighting or have a new electrical box installed to add lighting to a new area in your home.

DRIVEWAY PAVING MATERIALS

■ Since the driveway and the garage are so connected, upgrading the material used to pave the driveway can help the garage look better, too. The materials for paving a driveway can be broadly categorized into solid-surface and aggregate-surface. Solid-surface options include asphalt and concrete. Aggregate-surface driveway paving materials are typically gravel or crushed stone. Somewhere in between these two are pavers, brick, and stone.

Asphalt. Asphalt (top photo) has a number of advantages over concrete. First of all, it's a lot cheaper than concrete. Second, it is less prone to frost heave and, unlike concrete, it can be relayered. Its biggest disadvantage is that asphalt requires regular maintenance: Most asphalt driveways will benefit from an annual coat of sealant.

Concrete. Although more expensive than asphalt, a concrete driveway (middle photo) can be stamped and colored to improve its appearance. Concrete as a material is much tougher than asphalt, but it is prone to cracking from frost heave. That's why it's so important to lay a proper foundation for the concrete, install adequate expansion joints, and reinforce it with rebar. All of this generally calls for a licensed concrete contractor. As with asphalt, concrete should be resealed periodically to help it stand up to the elements and the constant abuse of vehicle traffic.

Brick. A brick, paver, or stone driveway when installed properly not only looks great, but can also rival the smoothness of a solid-surface driveway. This is particularly possible when interlocking pavers are used. The downside to brick, stone, and pavers is that underlying vegetation tends to grow up between the individual pieces, even when landscaping cloth has been installed over a properly prepared foundation of pea gravel or sand. Additionally, heavy vehicles can press individual pieces below adjacent pieces, resulting in an uneven surface.

3

GARAGE SYSTEMS

Will you do your garage makeover work yourself? Or will you hire it out? Either way, you need to have a basic understanding of the different mechanical systems in your garage that can be affected by a makeover. Garage systems include electrical, plumbing, framing, heating, and cooling. Naturally, being savvy about these systems will help you to take on projects safely and well yourself. You'll also be able to understand the work or the costs involved when jobs are hired out.

Here's an example: Moving a window or door a few inches may *seem* fairly simple. However, electrical and/or plumbing lines in the walls will need to be re-routed, the ceiling and flooring will be disturbed, and ceiling or flooring joists may need to be strengthened. So the better you understand these systems, the better prepared you'll be to do the work yourself, or to budget for work and talk knowledgeably with contractors.

COOLING OPTIONS

■ Common ways to cool a garage include ceiling and whole-house fans, window air conditioners, and central air, as illustrated in the drawing at right.

Fans. A properly sized and installed ceiling fan is a great addition to any room. Not only does it add a touch of style, it also offers cooling in the summer and heating in the winter. That's right—heating. No, it doesn't have a heating element, but a ceiling fan set on low in the downdraft mode can actually help drive warm air from up near the ceiling down into the living space to create a more uniformly heated room. Whole-house fans do a surprisingly good job of cooling a house. These large fans are mounted in the ceiling and are designed to pull cool air though a slightly open window or windows in the house. For a whole-house fan to work properly, it's important that you open plenty of windows to allow for adequate air intake. If you don't, the motor will strain trying to pull in air it's designed to move and will quickly burn out.

Window air conditioners. Individual room air conditioners, if sized correctly to match the square footage of the room, do a fair job of cooling. However, they are noisy and can also be quite expensive, depending on use. The advantages of these units is that you can move them as needed to cool different areas of the home, and that you can take them with you if you move.

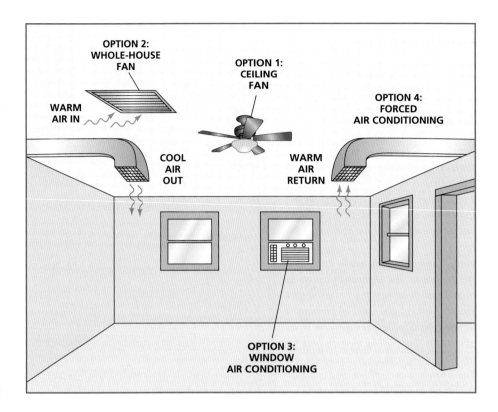

Central air. Central air conditioning units are typically mounted on the side of the house or on the roof. When mounted on the roof, they are usually combined with heating and are often referred to as "heat pumps" or "heat packs". With this type of system, cooled air is forced through metal ducting to various points in the home. Each room may have its own return duct, but it's more common to have only one or two strategically placed throughout the home. These systems do the best job of cooling a house, but at a cost: Summer cooling bills can be quite expensive.

Real Makeover Examples

ORIGINAL CARPORT

ENCLOSED CARPORT

MECHANIC'S DREAM BEFORE

MECHANIC'S DREAM MAKEOVER

For the real-life garage makeovers in this book, we started by transforming the bare carport of a 1980 ranch home into a fully enclosed garage. Then, we created five of the most sought-after "themed" makeover projects that homeowners crave: a Mechanic's Dream garage, a Craft Room, a Workshop, a New Living Space, and a garage that's All About Storage.

But we're not suggesting that you duplicate our makeovers. Consider them starting points—and, we hope, inspiration—for your own projects, guided by your needs, taste, and budget.

Each of the makeovers includes photos of the subject rooms "before" and "after," and a list of projects we did for the makeover, along with approximate costs. Maybe you'll get a design idea here...knowledge of helpful new products there...and maybe some do-it-yourself technique tips. There's room in every project for your personal choices.

Once you "shop" these pages for ideas and real-world inspiration, move on to Part 3: *Creating Your New Look.*

ORIGINAL CARPORT

This was our starting point: a single-car carport that was as bland as the house. The interior walls were covered with hardwood siding to match the home's exterior. The entry door led into the laundry room attached to the kitchen.

A battered, single overhead fixture provided the only light, and there was a lone electrical outlet along the long wall. The concrete slab was cracked, pitted, and stained...overall, a challenge that added up to real opportunity.

ENCLOSING A CARPORT

■ Same house, same angle—but what a difference! With a couple of new walls, a handsome garage door, and some paint, the exterior transformation is dramatic.

We started our Carport conversion by framing the two new exterior walls; we left openings for an entry door, window, and garage door. Then we wrapped the exterior walls with a vapor retarder and installed the entry door and window. Exterior sheathing went on next, followed by trim and paint. We insulated the exterior walls with fiberglass insulation to keep the garage warm in the winter and cool in the summer, and finished with a new garage door and opener. The result: For a modest investment, we added big value and convenience to the home. At this point, the garage interior can be renovated to suit individual needs.

WHAT WE DID

Framed exterior walls ($300)
Installed the following:
    Entry door ($150)
    Door lockset ($50)
    Double-hung window ($150)
    Garage door ($1,500)
    Garage door opener ($250)
Sheathed exterior walls ($300)
Trimmed exterior walls ($100)
Painted exterior walls ($200)
Insulated exterior walls ($150)
Total cost: $3,000–$6,000, depending on materials selected and size of garage

MECHANIC'S DREAM

For the Mechanic's Dream makeover, we used a different garage, mainly because we were so taken with the homeowner's car—a stunning 1941 Chevrolet Deluxe Club Coupe. Like most folks' garages, the original space (photo below) was cluttered and ordinary. These two elements made it the perfect site for the Mechanic's Dream makeover. The homeowner had spent over 10 years lovingly restoring the coupe to its original factory condition. Back in 1941, this top-of-the-line beauty retailed for $875; restored as you see it, it's conservatively valued at over $20,000.

The homeowner wanted a suitably handsome work space, but it also had to be highly functional. That's why we decided on three hardworking and practical but still attractive materials for the makeover: pegboard with the look of brushed stainless steel from DPI, Inc. (www.decpanels.com), colorful RaceDeck flooring (www.racedeck.com), and sturdy Hot Rod Garage by Sauder (www.hotrodbysauder.com).

WHAT WE DID

Installed the following:

Metallic pegboard paneling ($250–$450)

Triton pegboard spacer kits ($100–$200)

RaceDeck modular flooring ($900–$2,000)

Hot Rod cabinets by Sauder ($2,000–$3,000)

Total cost: $3,250–$5,650, depending on materials selected and size of garage

CRAFT ROOM

What crafter wouldn't love an organized, good-looking space to make projects easier? This Craft Room makeover was the easiest to achieve, because we used quality materials that went up quickly. We started by installing acoustical ceiling tiles to both beautify the ceiling and dampen sound. We chose go-with-everything 12" Washable White tiles by Armstrong (www.armstrong.com). Then we lined the interior walls with versatile storeWall panels (www.storewall.com). These panels come in 8-foot lengths and go up surprisingly fast. Next, we installed a laminate floor by Kronotex USA that looks like tile (www.kronotexusa.com). We choose their glueless flooring since it snaps together quickly with no mess. Finally, we added shelving and worktops from The Accessories Group (www.theaccessoriesgroup.com). A nice bonus about the worktops is that they're attached to drop-down brackets, so they can be stored out of the way when not in use. And the beauty of the storeWALL panels' flexibility really shines here: It's super-easy to move shelving and other accessories around however you like as your craft room needs change over time.

WHAT WE DID

Installed the following:

    Armstrong ceiling tiles ($250–$400)

    StoreWall wall panels
    ($1,800–3,000)

    Modular shelving ($500–1,000)

    Laminate flooring ($350–$650)

    DuraTop worktop and brackets
    ($475)

Total cost: $3,000–$5,500,
depending on materials selected
and size of garage

WORKSHOP

Do you need your garage to be a full-time, wall-to-wall workshop? Or will you share the space with a car? In either case, the projects in our Workshop makeover will get the job done. We started by sheathing two interior walls with drywall and the other two with T1-11 siding. T1-11 siding is perfect for workshop walls for a couple of reasons: It's tough and won't ding and dent like drywall, and you can mount items on the wall anywhere you want without having to hunt for wall studs. With the walls covered, we turned our attention to making a wall-mounted storage system. It's easy to make (see pages 172–175), inexpensive, and sturdy. Next, we mounted a variety of modular storage racks from Racor's InterChange line (www.racorinc.com) to the T1-11 walls to securely hold specialty items. Finally, we finished off the makeover by literally rolling out flooring manufactured by Better Life Technology, LLC (www.bltllc.com). Not only does this flooring go down quickly and look great, it also provides an anti-fatigue feature that your legs will appreciate after a day in the shop.

WHAT WE DID

Sheathed two walls with drywall ($200)
Painted exposed drywall ($50)
Sheathed two walls with T1-11 siding ($400)
Installed the following:
    Shop-made wall storage ($200)
    Racor InterChange storage ($75–$150)
    BLT Roll-Out Flooring ($600–$1,200)
Total cost: $1,500–2,500, depending on materials selected and size of garage

A NEW LIVING SPACE

When the house is full and you need an extra bedroom…family room…game room…the garage is a natural and popular choice. The big question is, do you want this conversion to be temporary or permanent? There's more than your present need involved—you'll also want to consider the future resale value of your home. Although the extra space may be a plus for you, many homebuyers want a garage. If you decide on a temporary conversion, consider erecting an insulated wall inside the garage close to the garage door. This way, you can remove the wall to easily reconvert the living space back to a garage at a later date. Alternatively, you can remove the garage door and frame in the door opening to make a permanent conversion, as we did here.

After we framed in the door opening and installed drywall, we painted the walls. Next, we laid easy-to-install vinyl tiles. Final touches included new overhead lighting (we used track lighting), and wall panels and accessories from Grid Iron (www.gridironusa.com). Although Grid Iron's sturdy, customizable wall panel system is designed for heavy-duty storage, we found it so attractive that we used it for the built-in entertainment center shown here.

WHAT WE DID

Framed the garage door opening ($100)

Sheathed and trimmed the exterior wall ($150)

Painted the exterior wall ($25)

Insulated the exterior wall ($50)

Sheathed the interior wall with drywall ($100)

Painted interior walls ($50)

Installed the following:

  Vinyl floor tiles ($200)

  Track lighting ($50)

  Grid Iron wall panels ($400)

  Grid Iron accessories ($475)

  Grid Iron workbench kit ($325)

Total cost: $1,500–$2,500, depending on materials selected and size of garage

ALL ABOUT STORAGE

■ If there's one thing homeowners want their garage to do besides shelter cars (and sometimes even that is secondary), it's to store things: bikes, garden gear, sports equipment, tools, and everything in between. That's why our final makeover is also the most-requested garage transformation—it's All About Storage. The problem is that without some kind of organizing system, the garage soon becomes a nightmare of clutter where it's almost impossible to find anything.

We turned to one of the world leaders in getting things organized—Rubbermaid—for our All About Storage makeover. We used their FastTrack rail and accessory systems, along with their sturdy cabinets (www.rubbermaid.com). The beauty of the FastTrack system is that all the accessories are designed to snap onto the rail. This makes it simple to rearrange holders, racks, bins, and shelving as needed. Just lift up the holder to disengage it from the rail, reposition it, and snap it in place. Once the FastTrack system was in place, we protected, sealed, and beautified the floor by applying EpoxyShield from Rust-Oleum (www.rustoleum.com). Finally, we installed the Rubbermaid wall and base cabinets.

WHAT WE DID

Installed the following:
   Rubbermaid FastTrack ($150–300)
   FastTrack accessories ($200–400)
   Rubbermaid cabinets ($300–500)
   EpoxyShield by Rust-Oleum ($60)
Total cost: $600–$1,200, depending on materials selected and size of garage

Makeover
Details

Hot Rod Garage by Sauder cabinets. Team up *Hot Rod* magazine and Sauder, a leader in ready-to-assemble furniture, and you get the cabinets designed and built to be a Mechanic's Dream (www.hotrodbysauder.com). These sturdy cabinets are both well built and attractive; they come ready to assemble and go together in minutes. The workbench shown here with overhead cabinets is designed to store the rolling island under the worktop when not in use.

RaceDeck flooring. It protects, it covers flaws, and it looks just plain great: That's the triple appeal of modular flooring like the RaceDeck product (www.racedeck.com) shown here. These easy-to-install tiles come in four patterns and an astounding 10 colors, so you can create the custom look you're after.

Gladiator storage bins. As part of our Workshop makeover, we installed a full wall of Gladiator GearWall panels (www.gladiatorgw.com) and filled them with open bins to organize and store the myriad pieces of hardware in our shop. By labeling the fronts of the bins, you'll always know what's where—and easily find what you're looking for.

Unfortunately, the garage fairy won't show up to cast a magic spell and give you an instant makeover. That's what this section is for—to show you the step-by-step techniques that will help you actually do the work and reap the rewards.

Do you want to turn your breezy carport into a snug garage? Give yourself some organized workspace? Create a versatile craft corner? Whatever your plans, we'll show you the how-to behind the makeovers. From finishing a ceiling to refinishing a floor, here you'll find the tips and techniques to get the job done.

We've divided the projects into the major categories involved: flooring, walls, ceilings, windows and doors, storage, and electrical. Each starts with an "after" photo showing the results of the tasks involved, plus in-process photos and a list of tools you'll need. The sooner you start, the sooner you'll have your own made-over garage ready to use and enjoy.

4

FLOORING

An ugly concrete slab complete with oil stains and paint drippings from the occasional home improvement project—does that sound like your garage floor? Happily, there's lots of help available. Today's market offers several flooring products for your garage that can transform the concrete beast into a beauty.

In this chapter we'll start by showing you how to clean and patch your old concrete floor so that you can apply any of the following treatments: paint, laminate flooring, vinyl tiles, epoxy coating, modular flooring, and roll-out flooring. Which one you choose will depend on how you'll be using your garage. If you're converting it to a living space, consider laminate flooring or vinyl tile. For a workshop or just a better-looking garage, try paint, epoxy coating, modular flooring, or roll-out flooring.

Cleaning Concrete

The state of your concrete floor will determine how easy or difficult it is to clean. Dirty concrete can be cleaned with regular household detergent. Stubborn grime can often be scrubbed off, but seriously blemished concrete requires an acid-based cleaner to remove tough stains.

Protect your walls. Regardless of the cleaner you're going to use, it's best to start by masking off any sensitive areas, such as adjacent walls. Cover these with plastic sheathing and secure with tape, as shown in the top left photo.

Apply the cleaner. Household detergent can be mixed in a bucket and poured directly on the slab. Chemical cleaners are best applied with a garden sprayer, as shown in the top right photo. Make sure to follow the manufacturer's mixing instructions and wear old clothes, plastic gloves, and eye protection when working with these harsh chemicals. Keep pets and children away until you are finished.

Scrub if necessary. For stubborn stains, use a deck brush or stiff-bristle broom to scrub wetted areas as needed to lift the stains, as shown in the middle photo. You may find it helpful to apply more cleanser or chemical cleaner as you scrub.

Rinse the slab. When the entire slab is clean, rinse off all cleaner with fresh water, as shown in the bottom photo. If you used a chemical cleaner, rinse the slab completely and then go back and rinse it again. Let the slab dry totally before allowing foot traffic.

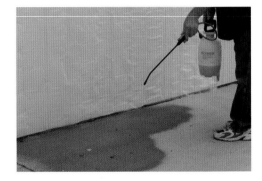

Patching Concrete

Even if it's been poured and maintained properly, odds are that your garage floor is cracked in some places and in need of repair. If the cracks are less than $3/8$" wide, you can fix them yourself with some concrete patch. Cracks larger than this are best left to a professional.

Clean cracks. To repair cracked concrete, start by chipping away any loose areas (make sure to wear eye protection). Use a hammer and cold chisel to gently clear away loose concrete on the sides of the crack, as shown in the upper right photo. Once you have the loose parts broken off, go back with a wire brush and clean out the crack, as shown in the inset photo.

Apply patch compound. Once the crack is completely clean, the next step is to apply a concrete patch. These come in squeeze tubes and standard caulk tube formats. Whichever type you choose, apply a generous bead to the crack, as shown in the bottom left photo.

Level. All that's left is to level the concrete patch with a mason's trowel, as shown in the bottom right photo. Use the trowel to feather the patch away from the edge to create a smooth surface. Note: If you don't have a mason's trowel, a stiff-blade putty knife will work just fine.

TOOLS

• Hammer and cold chisel
• Wire brush
• Mason's trowel

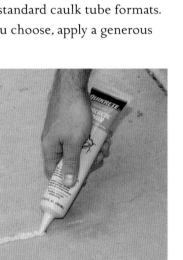

Painting Concrete

One way to give a garage floor a quick makeover is to paint it. It's important to note that concrete requires special concrete paint (see page 30). If you use ordinary paint, you won't get a good bond and the paint will quickly chip and peel off. Also, if traction is a concern, there are a number of anti-slip additives available for most concrete paint.

Prepare for painting. As with any painting job, the secret to success is proper preparation. Since a floor gets much more abuse than a wall or ceiling, this is especially important. For the paint to bond well with the existing floor, the surface must be clean and free from all debris. Start by sweeping or vacuuming the floor clean.

If you're planning on painting concrete, it's a good idea to clean the floor with household detergent or a chemical cleaner (see page 80 for more on this). If you choose to do this, make sure to rinse thoroughly and let the concrete dry completely before proceeding. You'll also need to deal with any cracks in the concrete before

painting. Hairline cracks (like the one shown in the inset photo) should be cleaned with a wire brush. Larger cracks should be repaired; see page 81. The final bit of preparation work before breaking out the paint is to mask as needed.

Trim around the edges. When the floor is properly prepped, you're ready to paint. Start by working around the perimeter of the floor. You can use a trim pad with built-in rollers, or simply brush the paint on with a foam brush, as shown in the bottom left photo. Paint out from the wall about 2" to leave plenty of clearance for the paint roller. It's also best to paint around any obstacles, such as columns and railings.

Roll the main floor. Now you can paint the bulk of the floor with a larger roller. You'll want to use a long-nap roller for painting concrete, since the surface is rough. Start in one corner and roll out about a foot or two, working along one edge of the floor (bottom right photo). Continue working in 1- to 2-foot strips until you reach the opposite wall. Take care to fully overlap your strokes to get even coverage. When you're done, allow the paint to dry completely and then apply a second coat.

Laminate Flooring

In the past, planks of laminate flooring needed to be glued together. Modern flooring, though—like the Kronotex USA (www.kronotexusa.com) flooring shown here—uses "snap- together" technology to make glue obsolete. The edges of snap-together flooring are molded to create a unique profile: There are ridges and valleys that, when mated, pull the planks together for a perfect joint. In most cases, this "mating" does require some persuasion in the form of a tapping block and a mallet or hammer.

Before you consider installing laminate flooring over your concrete slab, you'll need to do a moisture test. To do this, cut a couple of 2-foot squares of plastic and duct-tape them to various areas on the floor. Wait 72 hours and check for moisture. If you find beads of moisture on the underside of the plastic, you've got a moisture problem—call in a flooring contractor for advice. If the plastic is dry, you can install laminate flooring. Just make sure to first lay down a vapor retardant before installing underlayment. Also, it's important to buy your laminate flooring well before the intended installation date so the planks can acclimatize to the room. The

cartons of laminate flooring need to be placed in the room where they'll be installed 72 hours in advance.

Undercut molding. The first thing to do before installing laminate flooring is to undercut any moldings (door casings, etc.). Place a scrap of laminate on the floor and lay a saw flat on the flooring, as shown in the bottom left photo. Then cut through the molding; this way the flooring can slip underneath the molding and won't have to be cut to fit around it.

Install vapor retarder. In addition to a foam underlayment cushion (see page 84), most laminate flooring makers strongly suggest that you first lay down a vapor retarder over the concrete before installing the underlayment and flooring. For the Kronotex flooring being installed here, we laid down overlapping strips of 6-mil (0.2mm) polyethylene film. The manufacturer suggests allowing the film to run up the wall a few inches (as shown in the bottom right photo), and then trimming to length once the flooring is installed.

TOOLS

- Utility knife
- Installation kit (spacers, clamps, etc.)
- Hammer
- Electric drill
- Miter, saber, or circular saw

Install foam underlayment.

Before the flooring is laid down, all floors require some type of underlayment to serve as a cushion between the surfaces. Laminate flooring manufacturers offer a variety of options for this; rolls of foam are the most common. The subfloor should be level and free from dips and high spots. To install foam underlayment, place the cut end of the roll against the wall in one corner of the room and unroll it. Cut it to length with a sharp utility knife or a pair of scissors. To prevent tearing the underlayment as you work, most manufacturers suggest laying one strip of foam at a time and then covering it with flooring.

When it's time to join together strips of underlayment, butt the edges together and use tape to join the seams, as shown in the top inset photo; some manufacturers provide special tape for this; others don't. Make sure that the foam doesn't overlap.

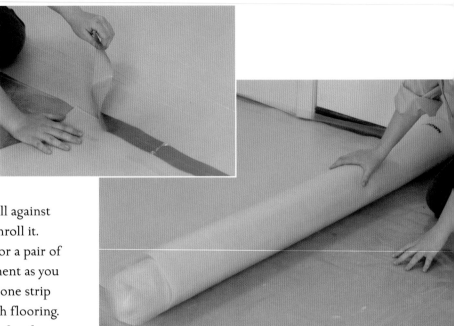

Lay down the first course.

It's important that the first course planks go down flat and straight so that the rest of the planks will be easy to install. Start by choosing the longest, straight wall as your starting point. Beginning in one corner, lay down a plank, inserting spacers between the plank and the wall to create the appropriate expansion gap. Most laminate manufacturers specify a $1/4$" gap. You can use scraps of $1/4$"-thick plywood or a combination of plastic spacers that come in an installation kit (which can be purchased or rented from most home centers). Push the plank and spacers firmly against the adjacent walls as tightly as possible, as shown in the middle photo.

Join planks end-to-end as needed.

Take care when joining together planks end-to-end: The narrow width of the joint plus the heft of the long plank makes it easy to break the fragile, profiled

edges. Snap together planks end-to-end, as shown in the bottom photo on page 84, cutting the final plank to length as needed. Note that it's important to stagger the end-to-end joints in progressive rows. Most manufacturers suggest staggering the joints by at least one-third the length of a plank. Typically, if you use the cutoff from the first row to start the second, the joints will be staggered correctly.

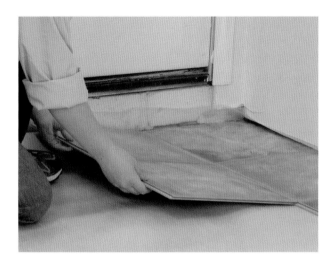

Install the second course. With the first course in place, you can start installing the second course, as shown in the photo above. As you slide each piece to mate with the previous row, use the tapping block (the one that came with the installation kit) and a hammer or mallet to force the planks together and tighten up the joints. To do this, slip the profiled edge of the tapping block over the tongue of the plank. Then tap it gently with a hammer; slide the block along the plank, tapping as you go until any gaps close up. You can use the block on the ends of the planks as well. As you work your way around the room, you'll most likely need to trim a few planks to fit around obstacles. Whenever possible, use a framing square or straightedge and mark directly onto the plank so you can cut it to fit. Laminate flooring is easy to trim with a circular or saber saw. Circular saws will cut best when fitted with a carbide-tipped bit.

Trim vapor retarder. Once all the laminate flooring has been installed, go back around the perimeter of the room and use a sharp utility knife to trim away the excess vapor retarder that runs up the wall, as shown in the top photo.

Add cove base. All that's left is to work around the perimeter of the room, installing molding to conceal the expansion gap between the flooring and the walls. For our garage makeover, we went with flexible cove base and attached it to the walls with cove base adhesive, as shown in the bottom photo. Alternatively, you can cut and attach solid-wood molding ($3/4$" round works well for this) to conceal the expansion gap.

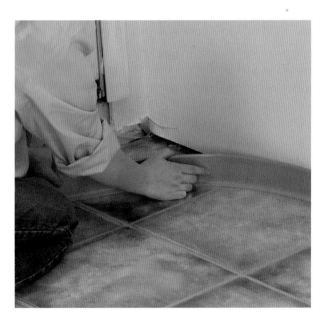

Vinyl Tiles

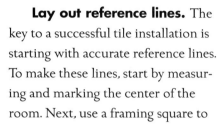

Peel-and-stick tiles, also called self-adhesive vinyl tiles, are simple to install. You just peel off the protective paper backing and press the tile in place. It really is that easy. Outside of a rented flooring roller that you'll use to ensure a good bond between the tiles and the subfloor, you won't need any specialized tools. Vinyl tiles are one of the easiest flooring materials to cut—all it takes is a utility knife or scissors.

One important requirement for this type of flooring is that the subfloor be flat, level, and free from dirt. Cleanliness is extremely important with self-adhesive tiles: Even the tiniest bit of dirt can contaminate the bond, resulting in a weakly attached tile. That's why we recommend that you don't apply vinyl tiles directly to concrete. The rough, porous (and usually dirty) surface will not permit a good bond, and tiles will quickly become loose. Instead, it's best to first install a layer of $1/4"$ plywood underlayment ($1/4"$ Lauan works great for this) over the concrete. Secure the plywood to the slab with a high-quality construction adhesive and concrete nails at the edges. Also, to prevent cracks in the new flooring, it's important to stagger the seams of the plywood.

Lay out reference lines. The key to a successful tile installation is starting with accurate reference lines. To make these lines, start by measuring and marking the center of the room. Next, use a framing square to lay out a line perpendicular to the first line, as shown in the bottom left photo. To make sure the lines are truly perpendicular, use the 3-4-5 triangle; see page 130. Measure and mark a point 3 feet from the intersection of the lines. Then measure and make a mark 4 feet from the adjacent side. Now measure from the 3-foot mark to the 4-foot mark. If the lines are truly perpendicular, the distance will be exactly 5 feet.

Test pattern. To keep from ending up with narrow tiles at the perimeter of the room, temporarily set out a row of tiles, starting at the centerlines you just marked and working toward the walls, as shown in the bottom right photo. If you find a narrow gap between the last full tile and the wall on either end, shift the appropriate centerline to eliminate it. Repeat this process for the opposite direction to make sure you don't have any narrow tiles on the remaining walls.

TOOLS

- Chalk line and tape measure
- Utility knife
- Notched trowel (optional)
- Framing square and straightedge
- Seam and flooring roller
- Hacksaw or metal snips for thresholds (optional)

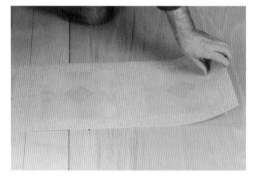

dispose of the backing. After all the full tiles are pressed in place, measure, cut, and install the border tiles. Self-adhesive tiles are thin enough to be cut with a pair of heavy-duty scissors. Don't remove the paper backing and then cut the tile; instead, leave it in place and make your cut. This way the tile won't stick to the scissors. If you're looking to cut a straight line, however, you'll be better off cutting the tile with a utility knife guided by a straightedge—just make sure to slip a scrap of wood under the tile before you cut (middle inset photo).

Peel-n-stick. To install self-adhesive tile, start by peeling off the protective paper backing (top inset photo). Then position the first tiles carefully along your reference lines, as shown in the top photo. Set the tiles in place and press down heavily with the palms of both hands. Place adjacent tiles so they butt firmly against one another. Work on one quadrant of the floor at a time. Note: Most tiles have an arrow printed on the back to indicate in which direction they should be laid. Make sure that all the arrows are facing the same direction as you install them so the patterns of the individual tiles will blend together correctly.

Flooring roller. The last and vitally important step is to firmly and evenly press the tiles into the subfloor to ensure a good bond. The best tool for this job is a flooring roller rented from your local rental center, as shown in the bottom photo. Thin tile can be pressed with a 75-pound roller; thicker tiles (such as rubber) call for a 100-pound roller. If you're doing only a small area, you can get by in a pinch with a rolling pin; keep your weight over the pin as you roll for maximum pressure.

Fill in a quadrant and cut partial tiles as needed.

Once you have one quadrant laid and the tiles are pressed into place, move on to the next quadrant, as shown in the middle photo. Note: Since you'll be generating a lot of waste with the backing, it's a good idea to have a helper handy to collect and

Epoxy Coating Systems

Epoxy coatings are either water-based or solvent-based. The water-based systems tend to be more user-friendly and more forgiving than solvent-based coatings, and they clean up a whole lot easier.

We used a coating system from Rust-Oleum (www.rustoleum.com) called EpoxyShield. An EpoxyShield kit comes with everything you need to get the job done; see the sidebar on the opposite page. The key thing to note here is that the quality of the bond between the concrete and the coating depends almost solely on how well the floor is prepped before applying the coating; make sure to follow the manufacturer's directions to the letter.

Scrub the concrete. We can't overemphasize the importance of preparation to the overall success of an epoxy coating. The actual application of the coating is quick and easy—what takes time and effort is the prep. Start by vacuuming the floor to remove all loose dirt and debris. Then mix up the concentrated cleaner, following the manufacturer's directions. Wet the floor with a hose, then spray on

TOOLS

- Garden hose
- Garden sprayer
- Scrub brush
- Squeegee
- Trim roller
- Paint roller
- Paint tray

Because garage floors take a lot of abuse, concrete paint (page 82) will hold up only so long before failing and requiring touching up or wholesale repainting. What you really need is a tougher coating than paint—something that will adhere better to the concrete. The answer to this dilemma is often an epoxy coating. Epoxy is a two-part thermosetting resin that forms tight cross-linked polymer structures. Translation: It offers toughness, strong adhesion, and low shrinkage; it is used especially in surface coatings and adhesives.

the cleaner. Then scrub an approximately 10-foot-square area with a stiff-bristle brush, as shown in the bottom photo on page 88. Make sure to keep the section you're working on fully wet as you scrub.

Rinse and dry. Rinse each section completely before moving on to the next section. Use a foam squeegee to remove rinse water from the surface, as shown in the photo above. Once all the sections have been scrubbed, go back and rinse at least once more; twice is better. You can also speed up things with a wet/dry vacuum. Allow the floor to dry completely. Then rub your fingertips over the cleaned surface; if you see any powder on your fingers, repeat rinsing and scrubbing until the floor is clean.

Mix the epoxy. Most epoxy coating systems come in two parts that need to be mixed together to activate the chemicals. Typically you'll pour the smaller chemical (the hardener) into the larger chemical (the resin). Stir the two together according to the maker's directions, as shown in the photo at right. In most cases, you'll need to let the mixed coating rest for a bit before applying it to the floor.

How long you wait—and how long you have to apply the coating—will depend on the ambient, or air, temperature. Since epoxy is thermosetting (sensitive to temperature), you'll need to take this into account when applying the coating. In general, the higher the ambient temperature, the quicker the epoxy will set up and the less time you'll have to apply it.

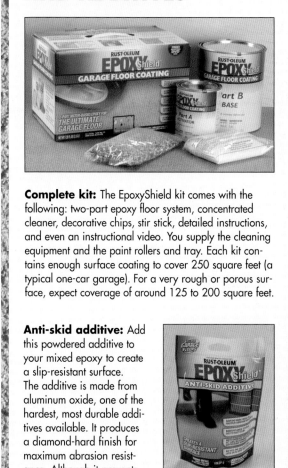

EPOXY KITS AND ADDITIVES

Complete kit: The EpoxyShield kit comes with the following: two-part epoxy floor system, concentrated cleaner, decorative chips, stir stick, detailed instructions, and even an instructional video. You supply the cleaning equipment and the paint rollers and tray. Each kit contains enough surface coating to cover 250 square feet (a typical one-car garage). For a very rough or porous surface, expect coverage of around 125 to 200 square feet.

Anti-skid additive: Add this powdered additive to your mixed epoxy to create a slip-resistant surface. The additive is made from aluminum oxide, one of the hardest, most durable additives available. It produces a diamond-hard finish for maximum abrasion resistance. Although it prevents slips, it's also gentle enough to walk on in bare feet. It's easy to keep clean and meets the Americans with Disabilities Act (ADA) requirements for slip-resistant surfaces. One package of additive can handle 1 gallon of epoxy coating.

Trim around the edges. When you've waited the recommended standing time, you can get ready to apply the coating. Start by donning a pair of disposable gloves, and remix the epoxy. Because you have a limited application time with an epoxy coating—especially in warm weather—it's best to have a helper to apply it. One person can trim around the edges with a small trim roller (like the one shown in the top photo), while the other follows behind and applies the coating to the floor; see below.

Apply the coating with a large roller.
Using a $1/2$"-nap roller, apply the coating to the floor with a large roller (typically 9"), in roughly 4-foot-square sections, as shown in the middle photo. To prevent lap marks, make sure to maintain a wet edge as you work from section to section.

Apply the decorative chips (if desired).
As you work in 4-foot sections, stop and toss the decorative chips onto the wet surface if desired, as shown in the bottom photo. Continue until the entire floor has been covered. The floor should be ready for light foot traffic in 12 to 16 hours; heavy items and heavy foot traffic, in 24 to 48 hours. For a full cure and vehicle traffic, you should wait seven full days before use.

Modular Flooring

If you're looking for covering for your garage floor that's both tough and great-looking, look no further than modular flooring. The modular flooring we used for our Mechanic's Dream makeover is from RaceDeck (www.racedeck.com). We chose this brand because it's the industry leader in modular flooring. RaceDeck flooring is made from high-impact copolymer to stand up to vehicle traffic, oil, grease, petroleum products, and most household chemicals. It's UV-stable and stain-resistant, and comes in a wide variety of patterns and colors; see the sidebar below.

One of the best things about RaceDeck is that it literally snaps together in almost no time. We went from concrete slab to finished floor in the Mechanic's Dream makeover shown on pages 66–67 in about an hour. It's that quick and easy.

There are two parts to the RaceDeck locking system: a female loop and a male loop. All of the tiles in an installation must have the female loops all pointing in the same direction. If you accidentally rotate a tile, you can simply pop it out and put it in the correct way. Always begin the installation in one corner, pointing the female loop in the direction that additional tiles will be added. RaceDeck also suggests that you start at the garage door and work your way toward the back wall. They sell transition strips that create a gentle ramp between the tiles and the existing slab (for more on this, see page 93).

COLOR AND PATTERNS

RaceDeck offers tiles in 10 standard colors: royal blue, alloy, yellow, orange, beige, white, graphite, black, royal purple, and red (we used alloy and red for our Mechanic's Dream makeover). RaceDeck can even make custom-colored tile if that's what you want. Pattern choices include traditional diamond for a metallic look; CircleTrac, a coin-top pattern; FreeFlow, which provides maximum air flow and drainage of liquids; FastDeck, featuring a hinge system that lets you roll up the flooring; and TuffShield, which offers a high-gloss, show-quality finish. Because each color and pattern is compatible with all the rest, you can mix and match to create a one-of-a-kind look. The possibilities are endless.

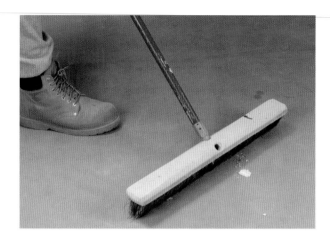

perimeter tiles will end up. To do this, start by butting a full tile up against one wall and then add tiles until you reach the opposite wall. If you'll end up with a narrow tile, consider splitting the difference between both perimeters. Yes, it's a bit more effort to cut tiles for both perimeter edges, but the installation will look a lot better.

Tiles snap together easily, as shown in the bottom photo. Just angle one tile up slightly so the male loops fit into the female loops on the connecting square. Then simply lower the angled tile and press down at the joint with the palm of your hand, as shown. You'll hear the six sets of loops engage. Occasionally, you'll come across a stubborn pair; persuade the parts to snap together by striking the joint with a closed fist. Do not resort to a hammer or mallet. If the tiles need this kind of persuasion, the loops probably aren't engaging properly; pull the tiles apart and inspect the loops for damage and then try again.

Clean the floor. Before you begin installing tiles, it's best to thoroughly clean the concrete slab to prevent dirt and debris from being trapped under the tiles. Start by sweeping away the bulk of the loose dirt and debris, as shown in the top photo. Then go back over the entire surface with a shop vacuum.

Test the pattern. Odds are that your garage won't be sized to match a full-tile installation—that is, no cutting required. To keep from ending up with narrow tiles along the perimeter of your garage, it's a good idea to lay out the tiles in a test pattern, as shown in the middle photo, to determine what size the

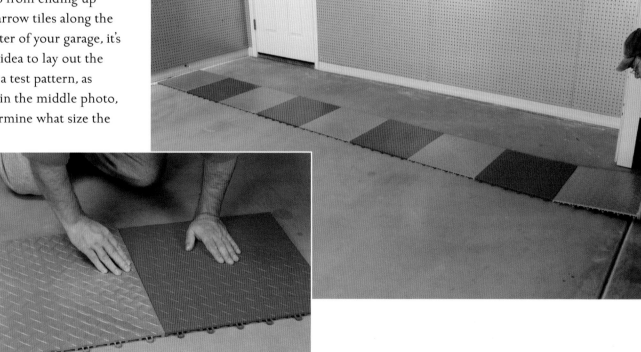

Lay the tiles. Once you've determined your pattern and have cut perimeter tiles as needed, you're ready to start. Lay down the first row, snapping the tiles together as you go, as shown in the top photo. Then move on to the second row, as shown in the top inset photo. The second row requires a bit more finesse since you're joining together two sides of each tile. We actually found it easiest to snap an entire row together and then join this full row to the prior row. If you try this technique, you'll find it goes much quicker with a helper (it's challenging to align the tiles along the full length of the strip by yourself).

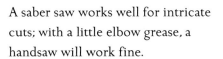

Cut tiles as needed. As you work around the room, you'll probably find places where you need to cut tiles to fit around obstructions. RaceDeck tiles cut easily with most portable power tools. We found that a portable trim saw gave us the best control and quickly cut through the material.

A saber saw works well for intricate cuts; with a little elbow grease, a handsaw will work fine.

Install transition strips.
Whenever you to need to make the transition from RaceDeck flooring to concrete, it's best to install transition strips, as shown in the bottom photo. These strips not only provide a gradual ramp between the different-height surfaces, but they also protect the edges of the tiles from damage.

Roll-Out Flooring

TOOLS

• Broom and shop vacuum
• Utility knife
• Straightedge

Of all the different types of flooring we used throughout our garage makeovers, we found roll-out flooring the easiest to install. The roll-out flooring we used is G-Floor from Better Life Technology (www.bltllc.com). BLT offers roll-out flooring in six colors and three patterns (see page 31 for more on this). BLT's flooring is 100% high-quality polyvinyl and comes in thicknesses ranging from 50 to 80mm; all of these help reduce fatigue, protect your concrete floor, and serve as a vapor barrier.

Because G-Floor requires no adhesives—you basically just roll it out onto your floor—it's a breeze to install. But what we really like about it is that when it gets dirty, you just pull it out onto your driveway and spray it down. You get a clean floor without water damage to your walls.

Clean the floor. As with any floor covering, the first step in installation is to thoroughly clean your floor to prevent dirt and debris from being trapped under the flooring. Start by sweeping away most of the loose dirt and debris, as shown in the middle photo. Then go back over the entire surface with a shop vacuum.

Roll out the flooring. Now you're ready to install the flooring. Because G-Floor comes in wide rolls (up to 10 feet in width), they can be quite heavy. So make sure to get some help. For example, the 10-foot-wide by 22-foot-long rolls we used for our workshop makeover weighed about 200 pounds apiece. Although two strong backs can often handle this, three is better. With the aid of a helper or helpers, move the roll into position near the back wall of your garage. Allow a couple of inches for trimming and then simply roll out the flooring, as shown in the bottom photo. Use a push broom to push out air trapped beneath the flooring, working from side to side and from one end to the other.

Trim as needed. When you reach the opposite wall, cut the flooring a few inches long and then go back and trim the first edge to fit snugly up against the wall. We found that the best technique was to guide a utility knife against a straightedge, as shown in the top photo. Slide the flooring up against the wall and then mark and trim the opposite edge. Check the fit along the adjacent walls, and mark and trim these as needed for a good fit.

Seaming together pieces. In many garages, you'll need to seam together a couple of pieces of roll-out flooring to cover the entire floor. The long edges of G-Floor are profiled to allow for an overlapping seam. Because this flooring lies so flat once installed, you can leave the edges untaped, as shown in the bottom photo.

If you want to completely eliminate the chances of tripping on a seam, it's a good idea to tape the seams. Just cut and apply a length of double-sided indoor/outdoor carpet tape to the bottom seam, as shown in the middle photo. Then simply press the top piece firmly into the tape to create a secure seam.

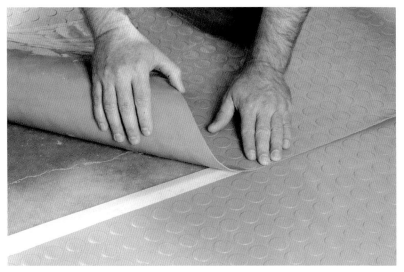

5

WALLS

Your garage walls may need just sprucing up...or a whole lot of work...or something in between. Like all home improvements, the amount of work—and money—involved depends on the scope of your makeover. You might need to simply paint the inside walls—or you might need to add new walls to convert a carport to an enclosed garage, or turn a garage into living space. Regardless of the project, wall work delivers a lot of impact, since it's the most highly visible surface of your garage.

In this chapter we'll cover framing new walls, installing exterior sheathing, insulating walls, installing and finishing drywall, painting walls, and installing pegboard and T1-11 siding to create abuse-proof interior walls. In short, we'll show you everything you'll need to modify both interior and exterior walls for your garage makeover.

Locate the mudsill. The first step in building a partition wall to enclose your carport is to locate the mudsill. Since the header is already in place, this is just a matter of transferring the header location to the concrete slab. The only decision you'll have to make is where to locate the new studs on the header. There are two basic options: flush with the header, or offset from the header. If the studs are flush with the out-side face of the header, you'll be able to run exterior sheathing all the way up to cover the entire header. If you offset the walls in from the header the thickness of the exterior sheathing, you'll run the sheathing up to the header and then cover this joint with a trim piece. Alternatively, you can offset the walls in farther from the face of the header and sheath and trim, leaving the header fully exposed.

Determine the offset (if any) and then use a plumb bob to transfer this location to the concrete slab. Hold the string of the plumb bob up against the header at one corner—the plumb bob will hover directly over the corresponding point on the slab, as shown in the top photo. Mark this location

and move the plumb bob to the adjacent corner. Do this at both ends of the header and at its center.

Lay out the mudsill. If you took your time with the plumb bob as described above, you'll end up with a series of dots on the floor. Use a straightedge or framing square as shown in the bottom left photo to accurately lay out the mudsill on the concrete. Do this for the entire length of both new walls.

Mark studs on the mudsill. The next step is to make the mudsill and top plate. Carefully measure each piece separately, as they quite often are not the same length (due to uneven existing walls). Transfer these measurements to your 2×4's and cut them to length with a circular saw, trim saw, or handsaw. Next, measure and mark the location of each of the wall studs, as shown in the bottom right photo. If the partition wall you're building has any openings for windows or doors, now is the time to mark them. For the utmost in accuracy, consider butting the mudsill and top plate against each other and marking stud locations on both at the same time.

Locate holes for the fasteners.

Once the mudsills have been laid out, you can attach them to the slab. For concrete, you can attach the mudsills with a powder-actuated nailer that "shoots" nails into the concrete, use lag shields and bolts, or use concrete screws (like Tapcons), as we did here. To do this, hold the mudsill in place and drill through the mudsill and into the concrete using a hammer drill fitted with a masonry bit, as shown in the top photo.

Drill holes for the fasteners.

As soon as you hit concrete, back the drill bit out of the mudsill and set the mudsill aside. Now go back and drill the hole in the slab to the required depth, as shown in the middle photo. Removing the mudsill like this allows the bit to more easily pull the concrete dust out of the hole and helps prevent the bit from overheating. With concrete screws, you should affix the mudsill to the concrete roughly every 12" to 16". Make sure to use a fairly stout screw (we used $5/16$" × 3") with a hex head to allow you to drive in the screws with a socket or nut-driver bit fitted in a drill.

Install a moisture barrier.

Even though we used ground-contact-rated pressure-treated wood, it's best to sandwich a moisture barrier between the mudsills and the concrete slab. This barrier will help prevent moisture from weeping under the mudsills. You can find rolls of foam moisture barrier at most home centers. Cut a piece to length so it's a bit overlong, and place it under the mudsill so it's centered from front to back along the entire length of the mudsill, as shown in the bottom photo.

end and secure the plate to the header, nailing along its length as shown in the bottom left photo.

Install the wall studs. With the mudsill and top plate in place, you can add the wall studs. Measure and cut one stud at a time, as odds are the header and the slab aren't parallel to each other. Cut the studs to fit snugly between the two—a tight fit helps hold the stud in place for nailing. Toenail each of the studs to the top plate and mudsill as shown in the middle and bottom right photos. If you've got an air nailer, you'll really appreciate how easily they handle this often-frustrating task (you can rent air nailers and compressors at most rental centers).

Attach the mudsill. With the moisture barrier in place, go ahead and secure one end of the mudsill to the concrete using the appropriate fasteners. We drove Tapcon concrete screws in place with a nutdriver bit fitted in an electric drill, as shown in the top photo. Move on to the other end of the mudsill, and before securing it to the concrete, make sure that the front edge of the mudsill is still aligned with the mark you made earlier on the concrete. Then install any remaining screws along the length of the mudsill.

Install the top plate. The next step is to install the top plate. Once you've cut it to length, attach it to the existing header. The best way to do this is to attach one end and then align the edges of the top plate with the reference marks you made earlier on the header. Once that's aligned, fasten the other

Frame any windows. Whenever you need to add a window or door to a wall, you'll need to frame a rough opening, as shown in the top photo. Stud placement is critical here for the window or door to fit properly. In most cases, the rough opening should be $^1/2$" to $^3/4$" wider and taller than the unit you're installing (consult the manufacturer's instruction sheet for the recommended gap). This extra space allows you to adjust the unit for level and plumb with shims. Headers for windows are most often placed the same distance down from the ceiling (or in our case, the existing carport header) as the header for a door. Although this isn't required by code, it usually looks the best and it simplifies both layout and construction. The other advantage to placing headers like this is that it makes it easier in the future to convert a window into a door since the header is at the correct height already for a door. For more on window framing, see pages 136–137.

Frame any doors. If the wall section you're building includes a door or doors, you'll need to frame rough openings to accept them. Cut king, jack, and cripple studs per your plan, along with a header for each opening. Attach the king studs between the top and bottom plate and secure the jack studs to these as shown in the bottom left photo. Place the header on top of the jack studs and toenail it to the jack and king studs. Complete the rough opening by installing cripple studs as needed (for more on door framing, see pages 140–141).

Add the exterior sheathing. Before you can add the exterior sheathing, you'll need to install a vapor retarder (see page 104) and any windows or doors. See pages 138–139 for instructions on installing a window and pages 142–145 for directions on how to install a pre-hung door and door hardware. With the vapor retarder and windows/doors in place, cut sheathing to fit and attach it to your framing as shown in the bottom right photo and described on pages 104–106.

Exterior Sheathing

The type of sheathing you choose for the exterior walls of an enclosed carport will depend on the exterior sheathing of your home. Most homeowners want to match the two exteriors so that the newly enclosed carport blends in with the rest of the house. Common materials are hardboard siding and exterior-rated plywood, like the T1-11 siding we used here. If your home is sheathed with vinyl or aluminum siding, you'll likely need to install a layer of exterior-rated plywood first to serve as a nailing base for the siding. Vinyl and aluminum siding can be tricky to install; if you want seams and joints that won't leak, hire a licensed contractor for this part of your carport conversion.

Install a vapor retarder.
Vapor retarders serve as a wind-breaker for your walls. They prevent moisture and air from passing into your home and causing problems, as well as preventing heating and cooling losses. They also help to limit moisture inside the house from seeping through the sheathing and deteriorating paint bonds. This is one of the reasons that paint on older homes fails so quickly—they don't have a vapor retarder. Although you can buy specialty vapor barriers (like Tyvek by DuPont), a heavy-duty grade of plastic sheathing will work fine. (Note: Find out from your local building inspector what material is code-approved before you buy a vapor retarder.) Cut the plastic oversized and attach it to the wall studs, top plate, and mudsill with a stapler as shown in the bottom photo. Once you've attached the plastic sheathing, you'll need to make cutouts for any doors or windows. The idea here is to cut the plastic oversized so that you can wrap it around the framing members to create a waterproof rough opening. Cut a square out of the center of the rough openings, taking care to leave plenty to wrap around the framing members, as shown in the

TOOLS
• Tape measure
• Hammer
• Circular saw or handsaw
• Straightedge or framing square
• Air nailer (optional)
• Utility knife
• Stapler

top left photo. At each corner, make a 45-degree cut that terminates at the junction of the corner of the framing.

Wrap and secure. Now wrap each section of plastic around the framing members and secure it with a stapler (middle left photo). Repeat for all four sides of the window.

Repeat for any doors. If there are any doors in the walls you framed, repeat the cutting, wrapping, and stapling procedure for each door to create a waterproof opening, as shown in the top right photo.

Install the first sheet. With the vapor retarder in place and the rough openings protected, begin applying the sheathing. Start by positioning the first sheet vertically at one corner so that its edge is flush with the corner framing. Check to see whether the opposite edge breaks the center of a wall stud, and shift the panel and trim as necessary. Attach the sheathing to the wall studs using 8d galvanized finish nails every 6" around

the perimeter and every 12" in the field. We used $1^{1}/_{4}$" galvanized narrow-crown staples and an air-powered narrow-crown stapler to speed up the job, as shown in the bottom right photo.

WORKING WITH FIBERGLASS INSULATION

■ Although fiberglass insulation goes up fast and easily, there are a couple of safety precautions you should take whenever working with it. Loose particles of fiberglass will irritate your eyes, nose, lungs, and skin (itching powder is often made from fiberglass). So it's important that you wear suitable protection: a dust mask to protect your nose and lungs, eye protection to keep fiberglass particles out of your eyes, and a long-sleeved shirt, pants, and gloves to protect your skin.

Attach one side. When using kraft-faced insulation batts with flanges (as shown here), start by pressing the batt into the cavity between the studs. Unfold one of the flanges and secure it with a stapler as shown in the top photo, centered on one stud every 8" to 12". The flanges can be stapled to the front or inside of the stud. Drywall installers prefer the facing to be stapled on the inside of the studs.

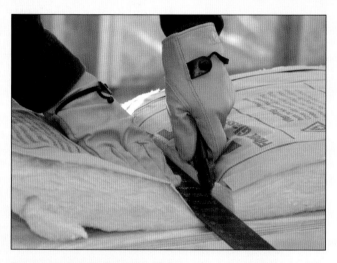

Cut insulation to fit. Even with pre-cut fiberglass batts, you'll find that you'll occasionally have to cut strips to length to fit into spaces above and below windows and doors, or to fit snugly around obstructions like electrical boxes, plumbing, and plumbing vent lines. To insulate properly, the insulation must fit snugly against the studs and completely fill the cavity to the top and bottom plates. We've found the easiest way to cut fiberglass insulation to length is to compress the insulation at the cut line with a framing square, as shown in the middle photo; then draw a utility knife along the square's edge to make the cut, as shown.

Stretch and attach the second side. Now unfold the flange on the opposite side of the batt and secure it to the opposite stud, as shown in the bottom photo. For batts being installed next to each other, it's easiest to secure both flanges at the same time with a single staple. This both saves staples and also creates less of a protrusion, which could interfere with the wall covering added later.

Installing Drywall

Many garage makeovers require removing and installing new interior wall sheathing. The easiest to install is drywall. We recommend $1/2$" drywall whenever possible, since it holds up better over time than thinner types.

Start in a corner. Start by positioning the first sheet tight in the corner and screw it in place.

Drive drywall screws or nails in so they sit just below the surface but don't break through the paper covering; see the sidebar below for more on drywall fasteners. The second sheet will most likely need to be cut to fit. There are two ways to do this: Measure, mark, and cut, or else cut to fit (see the sidebar on the page 110).

To measure, mark, and cut, measure from the existing sheet to the ceiling or floor on both ends of the panel and transfer these measurements to a full sheet. Draw a line with a straightedge or snap a chalk line, and then cut along this line with a sharp utility knife. Flip the sheet over and lift up one end to snap the sheet. Run your utility knife along the inside crease to cut completely through the sheet.

Secure around openings. As you work your way along the wall, you'll likely encounter rough openings for windows and doors. Secure the drywall to the framing members as shown in the middle photo. Alternatively, depending on the window or door, you may want to install corner bead to create a 90-degree edge that's protected. Mark and cut the metal corner bead to length. Place it over the edge and secure it with drywall screws.

DRYWALL SCREWS VERSUS NAILS

Feature	Screws	Nails
Ease of installation	Time-consuming without a drywall screw gun	Simple: requires only a hammer
Holding power	Screw threads hold drywall in place firmly; they do not move with changes in humidity	Poor over time as changes in humidity cause nail "pop," where the nail head protrudes from the drywall surface
Cost	More expensive than nails	Cheaper than screws
Ease of remodel	Screws can't be pried out, they must be unscrewed; takes much more time than nails	Nails allow you to pry off sheets; nails pry out easily to save time

TOOLS

- Tape measure
- Chalk line
- Straightedge or framing square
- Utility knife
- Drywall saw (optional)
- Drill and bits (if using screws)
- Hammer (if using nails)

WORKING AROUND ROUGH OPENINGS

Pro drywallers usually don't measure, mark, and trim drywall to install it. Instead, they cover the walls (including rough openings) with drywall and then go back and cut away the waste. Here's how they do it. It's important to note that this method does not conserve materials as well as the measure-mark-and-cut method, but it's much, much faster. That's what a pro is interested in—getting the job done as quickly as possible.

First saw horizontally. With a sheet of drywall firmly secured to the wall studs with screws or nails, the first step to removing the waste covering a rough opening is to cut the top of the waste horizontally with a drywall saw, as shown in the top photo. Yes, a drywall saw leaves a rough edge, but it doesn't matter since the rough edge will be covered with trim once the window or door is in place.

Next, score vertically. Use a utility knife to score one side of the drywall. Just run the blade of the knife along the inside face of the rough opening framing member, as shown in the photo above.

Snap and cut off waste. All that's left is to pull the waste section sharply toward you to snap the drywall at the scored line. Then you can go back and sever the paper covering at the break with a utility knife, as shown in the photo at left, to free the waste.

Finishing Drywall

Once all your drywall is installed, it's time to hide the seams and joints with joint tape and drywall compound, often called "mud." Joint compound comes pre-mixed or in a powder form that you can mix yourself. Once the tape is in place, a number of feather coats of mud are applied to make the seam or joint virtually disappear. When the mud is dry, you'll need to go back and sand or sponge it smooth.

If your makeover project involves installing a lot of drywall, consider renting a drywall sanding system like the Porter-Cable 7800 system. This system is a variable-speed sander with a built-in dust collection hose that connects to a high-efficiency vacuum. The business end of the sander features easy-to-change sanding pads of varying grits. The vacuum provides 99.85% filtration efficiency that's perfect for capturing fine drywall dust. The vacuum is automatically turned on or off by the sander's power switch. The vacuum stays on an additional 15 seconds after the sander is turned off to clear the hose. This combination of quick-smoothing action coupled with excellent dust collection makes even large smoothing jobs a snap.

Tape the joints. To conceal the joints between the sheets of drywall, apply drywall tape over the gaps. Drywall tape may be self-adhesive or non-stick. To apply self-adhesive tape, simply remove the paper backing and press it in place. Non-adhesive tape is applied by first spreading on a thin coat of joint compound over the joints as shown in the bottom left photo. Immediately, cut a piece of joint tape to length and then press it into the wet joint compound as shown in the bottom middle photo. Then grab a wide-blade putty knife and draw this over the tape to firmly seat it in the mud, as shown in the bottom right photo.

Exposed corners are best covered with metal corner bead—thin L-shaped metal that's easily cut with tin snips and is then either nailed or screwed to the framing members. Inside and outside corners are best done with special drywall tools designed especially for this; see pages 124–125. Apply the joint compound as smoothly as possible, but don't be too meticulous—you'll remove any high spots before applying the next coat.

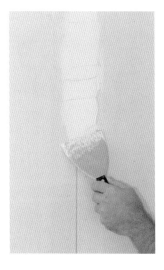

Fill the nail or screw heads. Once you've got all the joints taped, work your way around the room, filling the nail and/or screw depressions with joint compound as shown in the top photo.

Feather the joints. Once the first coat of joint compound has dried thoroughly (usually overnight), go over the joints with a stiff-blade putty knife and knock off or scrape away any high spots. Then apply the next coat. Use a wider drywall knife and spread the joint compound over the first coat as shown in the photo above. Work the

compound gently away from the joint to "feather" it for a smooth transition to the drywall. Multiple thin coats work best here. Let each coat dry, knock off any high spots, and then apply the next. Repeat as necessary to create a flat surface. At the same time, apply a second coat to all the screw or nail depressions. Typically as the joint compound dries, it shrinks and leaves shallow depressions that will be noticeable if they're not filled again.

Sponge or sand smooth. When the joint compound is completely dry, the final step is to smooth the surface to remove any remaining imperfections. This can be done with sandpaper or sanding screen as shown in the bottom photo, but tends to create quite a mess. A tidier alternative is to use a power sanding system as described on page 111 or to smooth the joint compound with a dry-wall sponge. Drywall sponges have a non-abrasive pad glued to one side to quickly flatten high spots. To use a drywall sponge, wet it and then wring it out so it's just damp. Then use a swirling motion to smooth the joints. When the drywall is smooth, roll on a coat of drywall sealer and then apply the decorative wall covering of your choice.

Painting Walls

TOOLS

- Paint tray and roller
- Trim pad
- Clean rags
- Foam brushes

Nothing works as quickly or dramatically as paint to make over a room. What's more, it's the least expensive decorative wall covering. You can make a drab space vivid, cool down or warm up a room with the right hues, define an accent area...the possibilities go on and on. Just stroll through the paint aisle of your local home center, and you'll be struck by the enormous color choices available. Thankfully, manufacturers make decision time a bit easier with sample color strips and design booklets (usually free) that advise what goes with what, and show how an unexpected hue could be just perfect.

Just remember: Dark paint shades tend to make a room seem smaller, while light paints open a space up for a bigger "feel." As to paint formula, it's usually best to stick with latex: It goes on easily and cleans up well. And a flat finish (versus gloss or semi-gloss) is the best look for most wall surfaces.

Prepare the walls. The first step to successful painting is to thoroughly clean the walls. Scrubbing a wall lightly with a sponge or brush saturated with a cleaning solution of tri-sodium phosphate (TSP) will quickly strip off dirt. Just make sure to rinse the wall completely with clean water when done. When the walls are dry, take the time to fill any holes or dings with putty (as shown in the bottom photo) and sand them smooth.

Then mask off any areas that will not be painted, such as window and door trim. Remove any receptacle and switch covers and tape over these as shown in the bottom inset photo; do the same for electrical wall fixtures or ceiling fixtures.

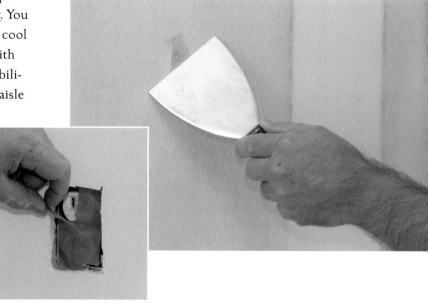

formulated to make the old surface more "receptive" to the paint. Priming also seals damaged areas and hides stains. And if you have the primer tinted to match the paint, you may need only one coat of finish paint.

Trim pad around obstacles. When the primer has dried, you can start painting by working around the perimeter of a wall. One of the best tools for this job is a trim pad with rollers, like the one shown in the middle photo. These also work great for painting around the edges of windows and doors. The only trick to working with a trim pad is to keep the rollers free of paint. Check the rollers each time you load the pad and remove any paint with a clean cloth.

Protect surfaces. Finally, make sure to cover the floor and any furniture with drop cloths, tarps, or old sheets, as shown in the top photo. Use masking or duct tape to tape the cloths or sheets in place or to wrap around obstacles as needed.

Prime. Even if the walls don't look like they need to be primed, do so anyway, as shown in the bottom photo. Primers help ensure a good bond between the old surface and the new paint. They're

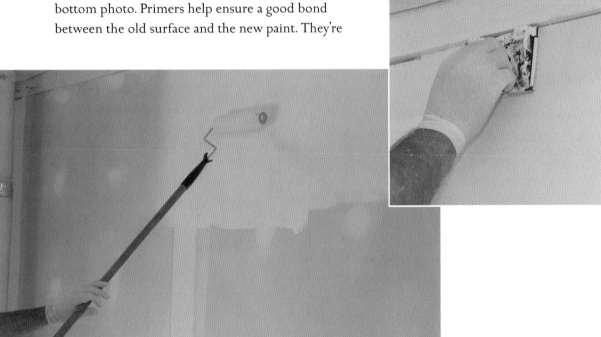

Small roller for corners. Small foam rollers like the one shown in the middle photo are great for working into corners. Since the rounded tip of the roller is foam, you can press it directly into a corner as shown. This makes quick work of painting corners and around window and door trim.

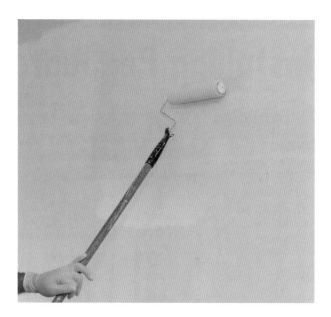

Roller for large surfaces. As soon as you've painted the perimeter of the wall, fill in the large spaces with paint as shown in the top right photo. Use a standard roller fitted with a disposable sleeve for this. The recommended standard sleeve is a 9"-wide sleeve with a $3/8$" nap. This will handle most surfaces and will lay a smooth, even coat. Rougher-textured walls will require a longer nap. A longer nap not only holds more paint that the rougher surfaces will need, but the longer nap can also get into nooks and crannies that a shorter-nap sleeve can't. Work in approximately 3-foot-square areas at a time and take care to keep a wet edge along the perimeter of the area you're painting to prevent lap marks.

Striking off. After you've rolled paint on a wall to cover it completely, go back and do what's called "striking off." Take your roller and begin at the top of the wall and roll it all the way to the bottom in a continuous stroke, as shown in the bottom photo. This will remove any roller marks and leave you with a smooth, clean wall.

6

CEILINGS

U nless we spot a leak or an insect, most of us ignore our ceilings, and that's okay for many rooms in a home. In a garage, though, the ceiling may have to stand up to an extra measure of abuse. For example, consider a garage converted to a workshop. Imagine swinging around an 8-foot long 2×4 and accidentally hitting the ceiling. If the ceiling is drywall, you'll end up with a big gouge at best, and possibly a hole in the ceiling at worst. Another ceiling factor is noise: A garage converted to a workshop or family room can transmit quite a racket to the rest of the home.

In this chapter, we'll show you how to protect a ceiling and how to install acoustical tile to dampen sound, provide some insulation, and beautify your new space. We'll also show you how to cover an exposed-joist ceiling with drywall, including how to finish and paint it.

Drywalling a Ceiling

The quickest and most economical way to close in a garage ceiling is to install drywall. But unlike in drywalling walls, gravity is working against you—holding the sheets in place over your head is both physically demanding and a bit of a challenge. This is definitely a job that requires helpers: at least one, and preferably two.

Also, make sure to use $1/2$"-thick drywall here, as thinner drywall will sag. If you're planning on blowing in insulation on top of the drywall (as we did), you may want to install a double layer to create a stiffer ceiling that won't sag. Blown-in cellulose tends to be heavier than fiberglass insulation, which does not require a double layer of drywall to support it.

When drywalling a ceiling, you'll want to install the sheet perpendicular to the ceiling joists, as shown in the drawing on the opposite page. This allows for the best screwing or nailing surface. Drywall comes in 4×8 and 4×12 sheets; unless you have several helpers on hand, we recommend using the shorter 4×8 sheets for easier handling. Finally, as an alternative to holding sheets of drywall over your head manually, most rental centers carry a nifty tool called a drywall lift. To use one of these you place a sheet of drywall on top and then crank the lift up until it presses the drywall against the ceiling.

Position the first sheet. It's best to start drywalling in one corner of the garage. With help, lift a sheet of drywall up and press it up against the ceiling joists. If you don't have a drywall jack, con-

TOOLS

- Straightedge
- Utility knife
- Wide-blade putty knife
- Corner tools
- Drywall jacks (shop-made)
- Drywall lift (optional)
- Driver/drill and bits

SHOP-MADE DRYWALL JACK

A drywall jack is simple to make and easy to use. The jack consists of a handle, a top, and two braces, as illustrated in the drawing below. The top is 4 feet long. To determine the length of the handle, first measure from the concrete slab to the bottom of your ceiling joists; then add $1^1/2$" to this measurement and cut a handle to length. We generally use a 1×4 for this, as it's rigid but much lighter than using a 2×4. All of the parts are joined with $1^1/4$" screws. When you build the brace, take care to position the top perpendicular to the handle to keep from having to angle the handle to pinch a drywall sheet in place. You want the handle of the jack to be perpendicular to the ceiling. If you were to angle the handle, when you pinch the drywall in place, the handle could work loose.

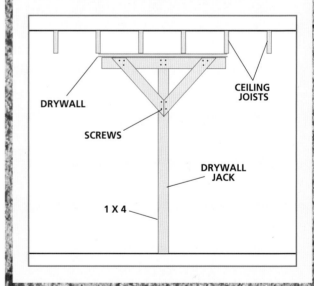

sider making a pair of drywall jacks as shown here and described in the sidebar above. Use the drywall jack to lock the drywall in place by placing the jack under

tension. The handle of the jack is cut longer than your floor-to-ceiling height. This allows you to wedge the jack between the floor and the ceiling to lock the drywall in place, as shown in the top left photo.

Attach the sheet. Once you have your first sheet of drywall positioned firmly against the ceiling joists, go ahead and secure it to the joists, as shown in the top middle photo. You can use drywall nails for this, but we prefer the extra holding power of screws. When drywalling a ceiling, we always double up on fasteners since gravity really wants to pull the heavy drywall down. Wherever we install a screw, we place two screws roughly an inch or so apart, as shown in the top inset photo. Double fasteners like this help prevent the tendency of the weight of the drywall from "popping" through the fastener. This is particularly important for ceilings, as joist placement is often 24" on center, versus 16" on center for most walls. And spacing the joists farther apart means the fasteners are under greater stress to hold the drywall in place.

Install the second sheet. With one sheet in place, you can move on to the next. Positioning this and the remaining sheets will be a bit more challenging than the first sheet, as you generally won't have two walls to press the drywall up against as you position it. Here again, you'll want to use drywall jacks or a lift to position and hold the sheet in place until you can drive in screws, as shown in the middle photo. Placement of the sheets is critical for a smooth ceiling; see below.

Offsetting seams. To get the smoothest possible ceiling when drywalling, you want to make sure that the seams of the sheets don't all line up. Instead, you want to offset the seams, as illustrated in the bottom drawing. This usually entails starting the second row of drywall with a half sheet, as shown in the drawing below. Offsetting the seams like this will help break up the long seam lines and make the seams less noticeable.

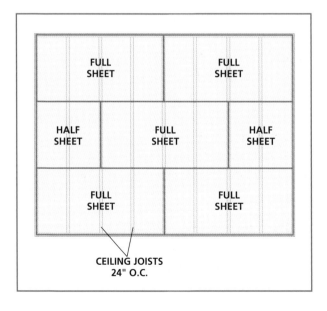

FULL SHEET		FULL SHEET
HALF SHEET	FULL SHEET	HALF SHEET
FULL SHEET		FULL SHEET

CEILING JOISTS
24" O.C.

TAPING CORNER JOINTS

■ Assuming that your walls are covered with drywall—or you plan on covering them with drywall—you'll need to know how to handle the corner joints where the drywall meets at 90-degree angles. To create a corner joint that looks like a single, continuous piece of drywall, you'll want to use some type of corner product (as described below) to bridge or fill in any gaps between the sheets.

Prepare the corner joint: For an inside corner joint using paper joint tape (as shown here), the first step is to apply a layer of joint compound to the adjacent walls, as shown in the top photo. This will serve to hold the paper joint tape in place.

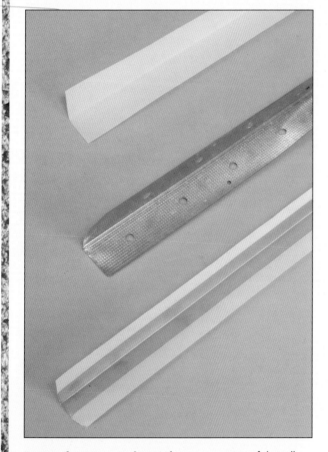

Types of corner products: There are a variety of drywall products available for you to choose from. All are designed to create a seamless corner joint. The three most popular corner products are shown in the photo above. From top to bottom they are: paper joint tape that can be folded in half and used for either inside or outside corners; metal corner bead, which works best for outside corners; and a combination of metal and tape that combines the ruggedness of metal and the application ease of paper tape.

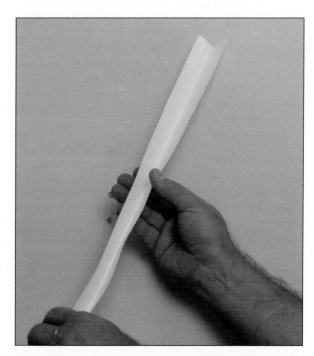

Fold the tape: Paper joint tape is pre-creased down the middle to make it easy to fold exactly in half. Just grip one end of the tape and fold the ends toward each other by pinching it between your fingers, as shown in the bottom photo. Then with your fingers closed tightly, pull the tape through your fingers. You can quickly fold long lengths of tape this way.

Cut and insert the tape: With the tape folded, now you can press it into the wet layer of joint compound that you applied previously to the adjoining walls, as shown in the top photo. All you're after here is to press the tape in place so it will stay there long enough for you to grab a corner tool (see below) and fully press the tape into the corner. Note: With a lot of patience and a light touch, you can install corner tape with a wide-blade putty knife—but it's a whole lot faster and easier with a corner tool, as described below.

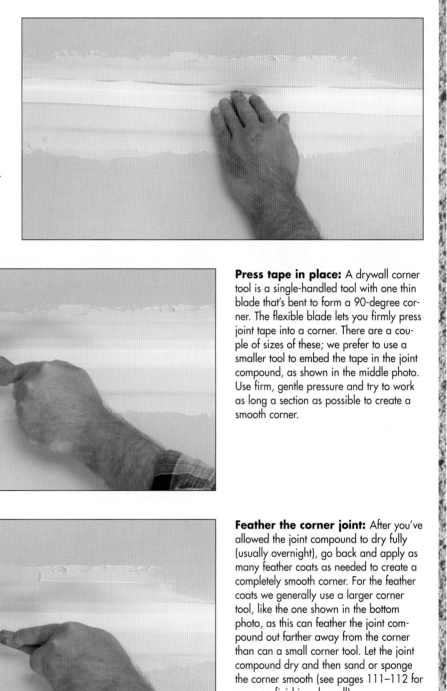

Press tape in place: A drywall corner tool is a single-handled tool with one thin blade that's bent to form a 90-degree corner. The flexible blade lets you firmly press joint tape into a corner. There are a couple of sizes of these; we prefer to use a smaller tool to embed the tape in the joint compound, as shown in the middle photo. Use firm, gentle pressure and try to work as long a section as possible to create a smooth corner.

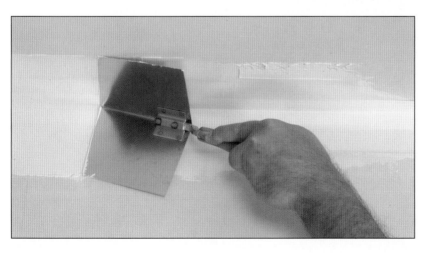

Feather the corner joint: After you've allowed the joint compound to dry fully (usually overnight), go back and apply as many feather coats as needed to create a completely smooth corner. For the feather coats we generally use a larger corner tool, like the one shown in the bottom photo, as this can feather the joint compound out farther away from the corner than can a small corner tool. Let the joint compound dry and then sand or sponge the corner smooth (see pages 111–112 for more on finishing drywall).

Painting a Ceiling

Whether you've installed a new drywall ceiling (see pages 122–125) or just want to dress up an old ceiling, the quickest and least expensive decorative ceiling covering is paint. Although you can use almost any latex interior paint for this, ceiling paint is specially formulated to be spatter-resistant and hide surface imperfections. By far the most common color for ceilings is white, since it goes with everything. But in some rooms, white can be a poor choice. White can actually make ceilings appear lower in rooms with low ceilings, and make them seem even higher in rooms with high, lofty ceilings.

Here are some general rules to follow when selecting colors for your ceiling. If your room has ceilings that are 8 feet high or lower, paint the ceiling a shade or two lighter than the color of your walls; this will help give an illusion of space to a low-ceilinged room. For ceilings that are higher than 8 feet, paint them a shade or two darker than your wall color; this can add a feeling of coziness to rooms with higher ceilings.

Prepare the ceiling. As with any paint job, your first step is to prepare the surface to be painted. For an older ceiling, take the time to scrub the ceiling with a stiff-bristle brush dipped in a solution of water mixed with tri-sodium phosphate (TSP), found at most hardware stores and home centers; rinse thoroughly. When dry, inspect the ceiling for dings and dents and fill any you find with spackling compound, as shown in the top photo. When the spackling is dry, sand it smooth.

Tape and tarp. The next step is to mask any adjoining areas with painter's tape, as shown in the bottom left photo. You'll also want to cover the floor and any furnishings with drop cloths or tarps to catch the inevitable drips and splatters.

Prime the ceiling. Even if your ceiling has been painted before, make sure to apply a coat of primer to the ceiling before applying the color of your choice. Primer acts as sort of an ambassador between the old paint and the new. Primer is specially formulated to bond well with old paint while offering a suitable surface for new paint. Bare drywall is best primed with drywall primer. Note that

TOOLS

- Putty knife
- Foam roller
- Paint tray
- Paint roller and sleeve
- Drop cloths

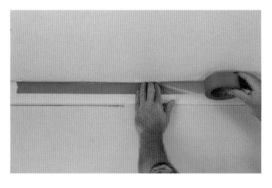

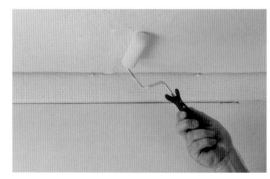

in either case, you can have the primer tinted to match your ceiling color; this will often allow you to paint the ceiling with a single coat, since the tinted primer helps obscure underlying imperfections.

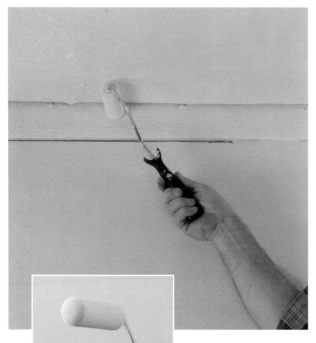

Trim around perimeter. Once the primer has dried completely, it's time to apply the ceiling paint. To do this, start by painting around the perimeter of the room. We prefer to do this with a small foam roller, as shown in the inset photo above. The advantage a foam roller offers over a conventional roller is its rounded tip, as shown in the top photo. The rounded tip lets you press the roller all the way into the corner junction of the wall and ceiling to get full coverage. It's best to trim-paint one wall at a time so that you can maintain a wet edge. This will prevent lap marks when you paint the adjacent area with a standard roller.

Paint large surface with roller. When you've trim-painted the length of one wall, stop and switch to a standard wider roller. A $3/8$"-nap roller sleeve will work on most ceilings. Longer naps are required for textured or porous ceilings. Apply paint in roughly 3-foot-square sections, working to maintain a wet edge with adjacent areas to prevent lap marks, as shown in the bottom photo. When you've painted the full length or width of the ceiling, go back and "strike off" the area. To do this, take your roller and, beginning at one end of the ceiling, roll it all the way to the opposite end in one continuous stroke. This will remove any roller marks and leave you with a smooth, clean ceiling.

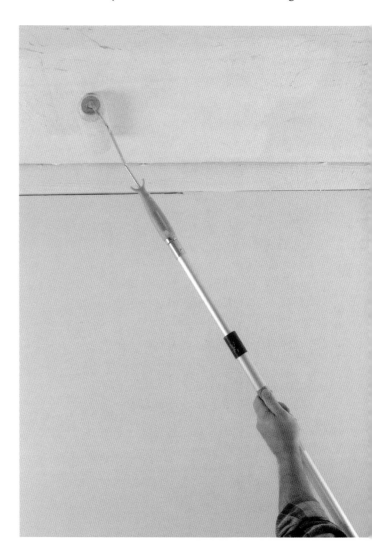

Installing Acoustical Tile

TOOLS

- Electronic stud finder
- Chalk line
- Tape measure and level
- Circular saw or handsaw
- Driver/drill and bits
- Utility knife
- Stapler
- Hammer or brad nailer

Acoustical tile is one of our favorite choices for a garage ceiling for several reasons. Not only does ceiling tile look great, but it also offers some insulating properties. Most importantly, it serves to deaden and dampen sound. This is useful in almost any garage, particularly those used as a workshop or as a living space, such as a family room. In either case the tile will quiet power tools or boisterous kids at play.

We chose 12" white textured tiles manufactured by Armstrong (www.armstrong.com). Armstrong's ceiling tiles can be mounted directly to an existing ceiling with adhesive, or stapled to furring strips (as shown here). In either case, the keys to a successful installation are preparing the ceiling properly and adjusting the tile layout to compensate for ceilings that aren't perfectly square.

Planning your ceiling. The first step to installing ceiling tiles is to plan the layout of the tiles. In virtually all ceilings, you'll find that you have to trim some tiles along the perimeter. For a balanced appearance, it's best if you end up with perimeter or border tiles that are the same width. To determine the size of these border tiles, start by measuring from wall to wall. Disregarding the foot

measurement, add 12" to the inch measurement, then divide this by 2. In the example below, the short wall is 16' 6" and the long wall is 28' 2". In both cases you'd drop the feet, add 12", and divide by 2, ending up with 9"-wide border tiles for the short wall and 7"-wide border tiles for the long wall.

Locate ceiling joists. We prefer to install ceiling tiles on furring strips instead of gluing them to the ceiling, since this allows easier removal in the future. To install furring strips, you'll first need to locate and mark your ceiling joists. Use a stud finder to locate each joist and then snap a line along its

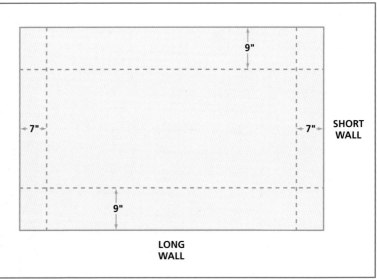

length, as shown in the top left photo. Ceiling joists should be spaced either 16" or 24" on center.

Attach furring strips. Once you've located the ceiling joists, you can install the furring strips. Install the first furring strip flush against the wall so that it's perpendicular to the ceiling joists, as shown in the top right photo. Nail or screw the furring strip to every ceiling joist. Place the center of the second furring strip at the border distance you calculated earlier, plus $1/2$" (inset photo at right). Continue to attach furring strips across the ceiling parallel to the first strip, 12" on center. For long or wide ceilings, butt furring strips under joists as needed and secure the ends with nails or screws; stagger butt joints to avoid having them fall on the same joists.

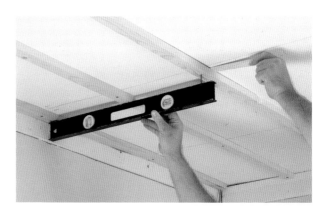

Shim furring strips as needed. As you work your way across the room, stop frequently and check the furring strips with a level, as shown in the middle photo. Insert wood shims between the furring strip and ceiling or ceiling joists as needed to level the furring strips; your new tile ceiling will only be as level as the furring strips.

Snap border tile location on furring strips. With all the furring strips attached to the ceiling or ceiling joists, the next step is to lay out the location of the border tiles. To do this, start at a side wall and snap a chalk line on the second furring strip at the border tile dimension, as shown in the bottom photo. Then "square the room" as described in the sidebar on page 130.

SQUARING A ROOM

■ Since ceiling tiles are square, you'll need to make sure that your ceiling is square. Most aren't. If you don't "square up the room" with the procedure described here, the tiles will end up crooked. The secret to squaring a room is the 3-4-5 triangle illustrated at right. This simple use of trigonometry basically says that if the three legs of a triangle measure 3, 4, and 5 feet, respectively, the corner of the triangle is exactly 90 degrees.

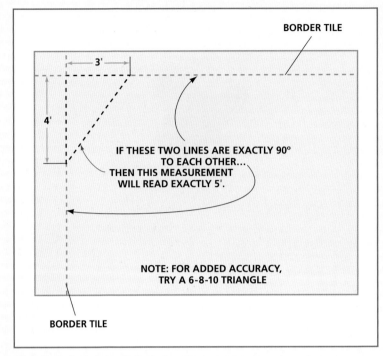

BORDER TILE

3'

4'

IF THESE TWO LINES ARE EXACTLY 90° TO EACH OTHER... THEN THIS MEASUREMENT WILL READ EXACTLY 5'.

NOTE: FOR ADDED ACCURACY, TRY A 6-8-10 TRIANGLE

BORDER TILE

Locate the sides. To use a 3-4-5 triangle, start by locating and marking both border tile lines on the furring strips as illustrated in the drawing above right. Then carefully measure out 3 feet from the corner of the border lines and make a mark as shown in the photo above.

Locate long side. Next, carefully measure out 4 feet on the adjacent border line and make a mark as shown in the photo at left.

Check for square. Now you can stretch your tape measure from mark to mark as shown in the bottom photo. If the tape measure reads exactly 5 feet, your two border lines are square and you can proceed with installing the tiles. If the tape doesn't read 5 feet, you'll have to shift one end of one of the border tile lines and recheck. This does take some time, as it's mostly trial and error; but if you skip this important step, you'll end up with crooked tiles.

Cut tiles as needed. With the room squared up, you're ready to install the border tiles. Before you can do this, you'll need to cut them to width. Acoustical ceiling tiles are easy to cut with a straightedge and a utility knife, as shown in the top left photo. Just be sure to cut the tiles face up to prevent the edge from chipping out. You'll find that it works best to take a series of lighter cuts, versus trying to muscle through with a single cut. When cutting border tiles, it's recommended that you cut them $1/4$" less than the border measurement to allow for variations in the walls; you'll cover any gaps later with trim molding.

Install first border tiles. Start in one corner of the room where the border tile lines intersect, and line up a border tile with both border lines. Then secure it to the furring strips with staples (top right photo). Staple each tile through the flange into the strip with $1/2$" staples. Install additional border tiles, as illustrated in the tile sequence drawing below right and shown in the top right inset photo.

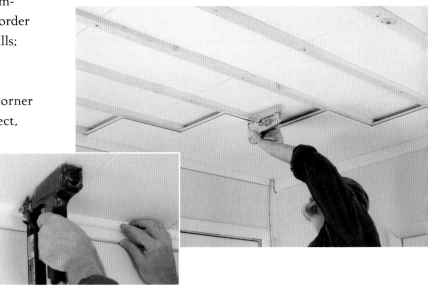

Install full tiles and trim. Once you've got the first few border tiles in place, you can start installing full tiles, as shown in the bottom photo and illustrated in the drawing at right. Continue adding border and full tiles until the ceiling is completely tiled. Finally, cut and install trim molding to obscure any gaps between the ceiling tiles and the walls, as shown in the bottom inset photo.

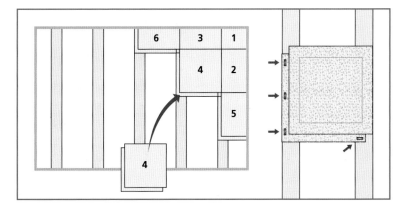

Protective Plywood

TOOLS

- Tape measure
- Chalk line
- Electronic stud finder
- Circular or saber saw
- Hammer or brad nailer
- Narrow-crown stapler (optional)

For garage makeovers where the ceiling will be taking a lot of abuse—such as a workshop, or possibly a family room—we like to install a ceiling covering that can stand up to it.

One of the toughest ceilings you can install is plywood. For most cases, $^1/4"$ Lauan will hold up well and look good, too. If you're planning on blowing in cellulose insulation on top of the plywood, consider moving up to $^3/8"$-thick plywood. You can install plywood directly to exposed ceiling joists or over existing drywall, as shown here.

Locate the joists. If the ceiling you're planning on covering with plywood has exposed joists, skip this and the next step. For ceilings that are covered with drywall, you'll need to locate and mark the ceiling joists so you can attach the plywood. To do this, start by using an electronic stud finder to locate the joists, as shown in the photo at right. Mark the joists at opposite ends of the room.

Snap chalk lines. After you've located the joists at each end of the room, use a chalk line to snap lines along the full length of each joist (as shown in the middle photo) to make it easy to locate them as you install the plywood.

Install the first sheet. Install the first piece of plywood by pressing it into one corner of the room. Although $^1/4"$ plywood is relatively light when compared to drywall, you may find drywall jacks handy to press a sheet of plywood in place so you can fasten it to the joists. See page 122 for more on making and using a drywall jack. To fasten the plywood to the ceiling joists, we used $1^1/4"$-long narrow-crown staples and an air-powered narrow-crown stapler, as shown in the bottom photo. Although you can use finish nails, a staple affords much greater holding power and tends to grip better over time.

Install the remaining sheets. As you work around the room installing additional sheets of plywood, make sure to stagger the sheets, as illustrated in the drawing below. Staggering the sheets like this will help break up longer seam lines for a smoother appearance. You'll probably need to trim a sheet or two to fit around obstacles or to navigate an out-of-square wall. Quarter-inch plywood is easily cut with a circular saw, saber saw, or handsaw.

Add trim if desired. Once you've covered the entire ceiling, you can add trim, if desired. You'll most likely want to use corner bead at the ceiling/wall junction to conceal any gaps between the plywood and the adjacent wall. Also, you can cover the seams between the sheets of plywood with screen stop or half-round molding, as shown in the middle photo. Attach the trim with finish nails, using a hammer and nail set, or install them quickly with an air nailer. Fill all nail holes with putty and then roll on a protective coat of satin polyurethane.

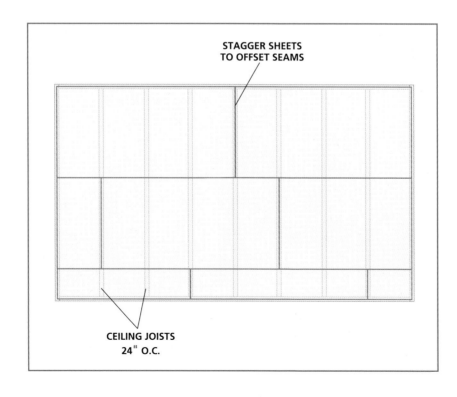

STAGGER SHEETS
TO OFFSET SEAMS

CEILING JOISTS
24" O.C.

7

WINDOWS AND DOORS

Picture this: windows and doors for your home. What came to mind? A graceful bay window? A gleaming wood entry door? Chances are that you didn't envision windows and doors for your garage, and that's too bad. Since many garages are connected or very close to the home, their appearance has a big impact on the overall appearance of the home. Consider, too, that your garage door is the largest door in your home and can have impact to match, whether positive or negative.

In this chapter we'll show you how to frame windows, entry doors, and garage doors. Then we'll take you through the installation of windows, entry doors, and garage doors, step by step. We'll even show you how to install and adjust a garage door opener. You'll find everything you need to spruce up your garage's highly visible windows and doors.

Framing a Window

TOOLS

- Circular saw or handsaw
- Hammer or air nailer
- Level
- Tape measure

If part of your garage makeover involves building a new wall or walls, odds are that you'll want to add a window or two. If you want to add a window to a wall, you'll need to frame a rough opening. Stud placement is critical here for the window to fit properly. In most cases, the rough opening should be $1/2$" to $3/4$" wider and taller than the unit you're installing (consult the manufacturer's instruction sheet for the recommended gap). This extra clearance lets you adjust the window for level and plumb with shims. Usually, the king studs are installed between the mudsill and the top plate, and the jack stud rests on the subfloor. So when you position the king studs, locate them $3^1/2$" farther apart than the width of the door: $1^1/2$" times 2 for each jack stud and $1/2$" for clearance.

The framing members for a window include king studs, jack studs, header, sill, and cripple studs. King studs are installed first, followed by the jack studs, the sill, the header, and finally, the cripple studs. Code in some areas allows for split jack studs with the sill sandwiched in between.

Note: If you're planning on installing a window in an existing load-bearing wall (see page 54) and you have to remove more than one stud, you'll need to brace the load-bearing wall with temporary supports. Temporary supports bear the weight that the wall normally would until a new support system can be installed (such as jack studs and a new header).

Install the lower jack studs. We used split jack studs here, as the carport header already supports the full weight of the roof. To determine the length of the lower jack studs, you'll have to do a little math. Since the top of windows are usually posi-

tioned to match the top of the doors in a home, start with 80" (standard door height) plus $1/2$" for clearance. Then subtract the window's height (our window is 36" high). So far we have $80^1/2$" less 36", or $44^1/2$". Now subtract the sill's thickness ($1^1/2$") and the mudsill's thickness ($1^1/2$") to get the length of the lower jack studs. In our case $44^1/2$" minus 3" equals $41^1/2$". Cut two lower jack studs to length and face-nail one of these to each of the king studs, as shown in the top photo.

Install the sill. With the lower jack studs in place, cut a sill to fit between the two king studs. Set the sill on top of the lower jack studs and secure it with nails as shown in the bottom photo.

Install the lower cripple studs. Now you can cut lower cripple studs to fit between the mudsill and the sill and nail them in place, spacing them 16" on center, as shown in the top left photo.

Install the upper jack studs. The next step is to cut two upper jack studs to length—these will be the height of your window plus $1/2$" for clearance (in our case, $36^1/2$"). Face-nail these studs to the king studs as shown in the top right photo.

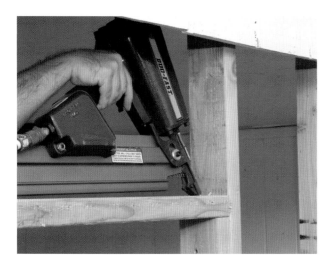

Install the header. Once the jack and king studs are in place, you can build and install the header that will fit on top of the jack studs. Since the wall we're building here already has a header in place (to support the roof), you don't need a load-bearing header. Instead, you can install a single 2×4 on edge as shown in the middle photo. If you are installing a window in a new wall that doesn't have an existing header, measure the span between the king studs and consult the header chart on page 32

to determine the width (height) of the header. Measure and cut the header components to length (typically two pieces of 2-by material with a layer of $1/2$" plywood sandwiched in the middle), and screw or nail them together. Then position the header and toenail it to the jack and king studs.

Install the upper cripple studs. Finally, you can install cripple studs between the header and top plate. Measure the distance between the two, and cut short cripple studs to length. Face-nail one to each king stud (as shown in the bottom photo) and then space the remaining cripple studs 16" on center and toenail them to the header and top plate. Note: Now it's safe to remove any temporary supports you installed earlier. Your rough opening is now ready for the window (see pages 138–139).

Installing a Window

Regardless of the type of window, the basic steps for installing a window are similar: You insert the window in the rough opening, shim it so it's level and plumb, and secure it. What's different is how you secure the window. Most windows for new construction come with flanges that are nailed to the exterior sheathing. Some windows don't have these and must be secured by driving nails through the sides of the window, through the shims, and into the framing members.

Protect the window. One of the best ways you can protect your new window—and the surrounding framing—is to install a vapor retarder as described on page 104. To fully protect the window and the framing members, wrap the vapor retarder around the front edge of the window and secure it to the inside face of the upper jack studs, as shown in the bottom left photo.

Insert window in rough opening. If you measured correctly and have framed the opening the correct size, the new window should slide in easily, as shown in the bottom right photo. You should have about $1/2$" to 1" combined clearance between the sides of the new window and the jamb. This space allows you to slip in shims and level the window; see below.

Shim it level and plumb. In order for the new window to operate without binding, it's important that the window be installed level and plumb.

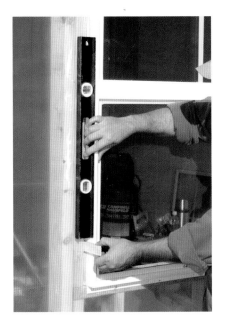

Check for this with a level on the sides, top, and bottom, as shown in the top left photo. Insert pairs of shims as needed in the gaps between the sides of the new window and the jambs. Slide the shims back and forth and in and out until the window is level and plumb.

Attach jamb to frame through shims.

With the window level and plumb, you can now secure it to the jamb with casing nails or screws, as shown in the top right photo. Make sure to drive in nails or screws only where the shims are to keep from bowing the sides of the window. Cut off protruding shims with a sharp utility knife.

Secure flange to exterior.

If your window is the type with a flange, go ahead and secure the flange to the exterior sheathing with galvanized nails, screws, or staples, as shown in the bottom photo.

Seal the window.

Since windows are installed in oversized rough openings, there will be gaps between the sides of the window and the framing. Although these gaps will be covered by window casing, the gaps can and will allow air to flow in and out of the house. To prevent warm air from escaping in the winter and cool air in the summer, you will need to fill these gaps. A number of manufacturers make special foam sealants for this, like DAP sealant (bottom right photo). Under no circumstances should you use standard expanding foam to fill these gaps. If you do, the foam can expand so much that it can cause the window to bind or to not open at all. The specialty foam window sealants use low- or minimal-expanding foam to get the job done. As a general rule, you'll want to fill the cavities about 75% full and let the foam expand into the remainder. Once dry, you can trim any excess off with a utility knife.

Framing an Entry Door

TOOLS

- Hammer or air nailer
- Tape measure and level
- Circular or miter saw
- Framing square

To add a door to a wall, or if you're installing a different width door, you'll need to frame a rough opening, as illustrated in the drawing on page 141. In most cases, the rough opening should be $1/2$" to 1" wider and taller than the unit you're installing (consult the door manufacturer's instruction sheet for the recommended gap). Whenever an opening is made in the wall for a window or door, a horizontal framing member called a header is installed to assume the load of the wall studs that were removed. The header is supported by jack studs (also referred to as trimmer studs) that are attached to full-length wall studs known as king studs. The shorter studs that run between the header and the top plate are called cripple studs. The extra space in the rough opening allows you to adjust the unit for level and plumb with shims. In no case should you frame the opening for a wider gap. If you do, the fasteners you use to secure the door may only penetrate into the shims and not the jack or trimmer studs.

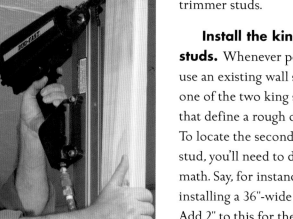

Install the king studs. Whenever possible, use an existing wall stud as one of the two king studs that define a rough opening. To locate the second king stud, you'll need to do a little math. Say, for instance, you're installing a 36"-wide door. Add 2" to this for the two

$1/2$"-thick jambs and 1" for clearance—this means your jack studs need to be 38" apart. Now add 3" to this (for the two jack studs), and your second king stud needs to be 41" away from the first. Measure over, cut a stud to length, and toenail it to the top plate and mudsill as shown in the bottom left photo.

Install the jack studs. Next, cut two jack studs to length; typically these will be $80^1/2$" (standard door height plus $1/2$" for clearance). If your mudsill extends out past the king studs and the jack studs will sit on top of these, subtract the thickness of the mudsill ($1^1/2$") and cut the jack studs 79". Face-nail one of these to each of the king studs as shown in the top photo. It's a good idea now to re-measure the width of the opening

and the actual width of the door to make sure it will fit in the rough opening.

Build the header. With the jack and king studs in place, you can build the header. Note: If the wall you're working on is a load-bearing wall, consult your local building code for recommended header sizes. If you're working on a partition wall, measure the span between the king studs and cut a pair of 2×6's or 2×8's to this length. Since the combined thickness of the two 2-by pieces is only 3", a piece of $^1/_2$" plywood or $^1/_2$" plywood spacers are sandwiched in between the 2-bys to create a $3^1/_2$"-thick header. Stack the header parts together with the ends flush, and screw or nail them together as shown in the bottom right photo on page 140.

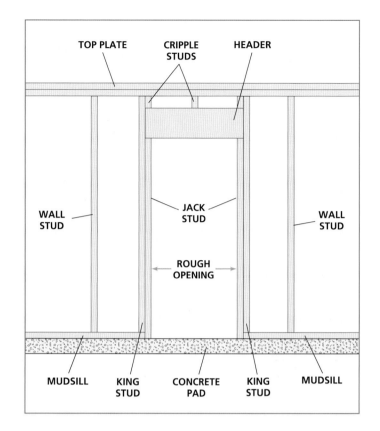

Install the header. Once you've built the header, lift it up and set it on top of the jack studs; if you measured and cut with precision, this should be a nice, snug fit. Adjust the header until its face is flush with the front and back edges of the king studs. Then secure the header by driving nails or screws through the king studs and into the ends of the header, as shown in the top left photo.

Install the cripple studs. Finally, you can install cripple studs between the header and top plate. Measure the distance between the two and cut short cripple studs to length. Face-nail one to each king stud, and then space the remaining cripple studs 16" on center and toe-nail them to the header and top plate, as shown in the bottom right photo. Note: With the door opening framed, it's now safe to remove any temporary supports that you may have installed.

Installing an Exterior Door

Pre-hung exterior doors use a special kind of molding called brick molding to cover gaps between the jambs of the door and the rough opening. This molding can come either pre-attached, or the way it's shown here, which you'll have to attach yourself. Brick molding is much thicker than interior door casing because it was originally used to provide an edge or stop for bricks to butt up against on homes with brick exteriors. Although it's used for all types of exteriors now, the name has stuck—along with the unnecessary thickness.

Apply caulk to the threshold.

The first thing to do before installing a door is to apply caulk to the threshold to keep moisture from seeping under the threshold. Use a high-

quality silicone caulk and apply generously in a zigzag pattern, like the one shown in the bottom left photo. Keep in mind that it's a whole lot easier to wipe off excess caulk than it is to remove the door after it's been installed and apply more caulk when you discover that the threshold leaks.

Insert door in the rough opening. With the caulk applied, lift the door up and into the rough opening to make sure it fits well, as shown in the bottom middle photo. Exterior doors tend to be rather heavy, so have a helper on hand to assist you as you lift and position the door. Once the door is in place, check to make sure you have sufficient clearance between both side jambs and the jack studs for the shims you'll use to plumb and level the door.

Shim door plumb and level. With the door in place, the next step is to add shims to level

and plumb the door. Start by inserting shims behind each of the three hinges, behind the opening for the plunger for the door lockset, and at the top and bottom of the latch-side jamb. Also insert pairs of shims at the center and both ends of the head jamb. Insert the shims in pairs of opposing wedges, and adjust them in and out until they solidly fill the gap between the jamb and the framing members.

Hold a 4-foot level up against one of the side jambs and check it for plumb, as shown in the bottom right photo on page 142. Finally, hold a small torpedo level up against the head jamb to make sure it's level. If any of these are off, the door won't open or close properly. Take your time here and double-check everything one more time before proceeding to the next step.

Secure the jambs. Once you're satisfied that the door is level and plumb, you can secure it to the doorjamb. Your best bet here is $2^{1}/_{2}$"- to 3"-long galvanized casing nails. Make sure to drive the nails through the jamb only at the places where the shims are. The idea here is to drive the nail though the jamb and the shims into the framing members (top photo). This way the jamb will be fully supported. As you nail the jambs in place, check for plumb again with a level and adjust the shims as necessary. Also, most pre-hung doors come with three long

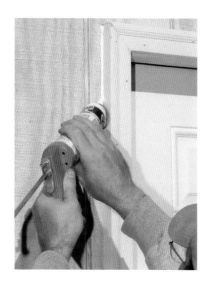

hinge screws that are designed to lock the doorjamb firmly into the framing members. The door hinges may or may not have an empty slot waiting for these. If not, you'll need to remove one screw from each jamb hinge and replace it with a longer screw. If your door didn't come with these, use 3"-long galvanized or coated deck screws and drive one into each hinge.

Secure the brick molding.
All that's left to secure the door is to attach the brick molding to the doorjambs (if not already installed) and to the framing members. Attach the brick molding to the jambs and framing members with $2^{1}/_{2}$" to 3" galvanized casing nails about every 12" or so, as shown in the middle photo.

Caulk around exterior.
Now go back and countersink each nail with a nail set and fill the holes with an exterior-grade putty.

There's one more job to do on the exterior of the door, and that's to apply a bead of caulk around the perimeter of the brick molding. Use a high-quality paintable silicone caulk and apply a generous bead where the brick molding meets the siding, as shown in the bottom photo. Fill in any gaps as needed with the caulk and then go back over the caulk with a wet fingertip to smooth it out.

Installing Door Hardware

TOOLS

- Drill and bits
- Screwdriver
- Chisel (optional)

The ease with which you can install a new lockset depends on a couple of things. If you're simply replacing an old lockset and the new unit is sized the same, just reverse the order of disassembly to install the new unit; see the drawing on the opposite page. As long as the hole sizes are the same, most new locksets let you adjust the length of the plunger to compensate for differences in the offset—that is, the distance the large hole is from the edge of the door. If you insert the plunger and find that the stem holes (the holes that the mounting screws pass through) are centered in the hole, the plunger needs no adjustment.

Install the plunger. The plunger fits into a mortise in the door edge. Most new doors are pre-drilled and mortised to accept a plunger. If your door isn't pre-drilled, use the template provided by the manufacturer to locate the hole and drill the recommended size. In some cases, you'll need to enlarge the existing mortise, or cut one to fit if you're installing a lockset in a door that hasn't been pre-drilled. In either case, just push the plunger in until the face plate butts up against the edge and trace around it with a pencil. Then remove about $1/8$" of material inside the marked lines with a sharp chisel. Check the fit by pressing the plunger mechanism all the way in. If the fit is good, drill two pilot holes to accept the mounting screws and install these with a screwdriver, as shown in the bottom left photo.

Install one-half of the lockset. With the plunger mechanism in place, you can begin installing the two halves of the lockset. Start by inserting the half that contains the actuator that passes through the plunger mechanism, as shown in the middle photo. In most cases, this actuator is keyed to fit only one way. Insert the tip of the actuator in the hole in the plunger mechanism and push the knob in until it butts up against the face of the door. Check the operation now by turning the handle—the plunger in the edge of the door should go in and out smoothly.

Install the second half of the lockset.

Next, install the second half of the lockset. Here again, the cavity inside the knob or handle will be keyed to slip over the actuator only one way. Align the cavity with the actuator and push the lockset onto the actuator until it butts up against the face of the door. Check the operation to make sure the plunger retracts and extends smoothly. Now you can secure the two halves together. Insert the screws in the holes in the lockset or retaining plate so they pass through the stem holes in the plunger and into the second half of the lockset. Tighten them with a screwdriver (as shown in the top photo) and recheck the operation of the plunger.

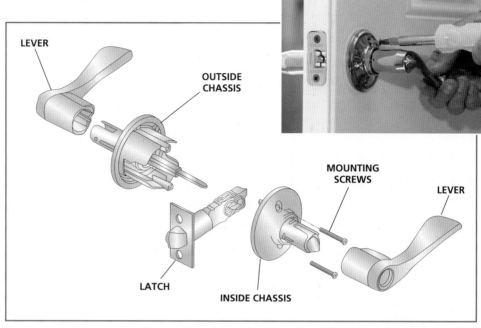
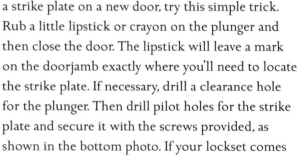

LEVER

OUTSIDE CHASSIS

MOUNTING SCREWS

LEVER

LATCH

INSIDE CHASSIS

Install the strike plate.

Once the lockset is installed, you can mount the strike plate in the doorjamb. For a replacement lockset, position the new strike plate where the existing one was. To locate

a strike plate on a new door, try this simple trick. Rub a little lipstick or crayon on the plunger and then close the door. The lipstick will leave a mark on the doorjamb exactly where you'll need to locate the strike plate. If necessary, drill a clearance hole for the plunger. Then drill pilot holes for the strike plate and secure it with the screws provided, as shown in the bottom photo. If your lockset comes with a deadbolt, repeat the installation procedure for the deadbolt (inset).

Lockset anatomy.

A typical lockset has three main parts: a two-section lever assembly and a plunger, as illustrated in the drawing above. One-half of the lever assembly usually houses the actuator—that is, a metal bar or tube that passes through the plunger into the opposite handle assembly. When either lever is operated, it rotates the actuator to pull the plunger in, allowing the door to open. The plunger mates up with a strike plate mortised into the doorjamb.

Framing a Garage Door

TOOLS

- Circular or miter saw
- Drill and bits
- Framing square
- Tape measure and level
- Hammer or air nailer
- Nail set and putty knife (optional)
- Hammer drill and masonry bits

Framing an opening for a garage door is similar to framing an opening for an entry door, with two differences: The opening is much larger, and it's sized to fit the door. That is, unlike a standard rough opening that's oversized to allow room for shimming the door level and plumb, the opening for a garage door is framed to fit the door. That's because the door doesn't fit inside the opening, it fits behind it. It has to sit behind the opening or it wouldn't be able to open or close via the door track. A weatherproof seal is created by installing rubber seals or stops along the inside edges of the opening (for more on installing a garage door, see pages 149–153).

This means you'll have to decide on a specific door before you start framing. Make sure to check the manufacturer's installation sheet for the recommended opening size. When calculating framing member sizes, and laying out their locations, make sure to take into account any trim work. In most cases, the inner faces of the opening are covered with trim pieces. This final, finished opening must be the recommended size for the door. For example, say the opening size you need is 108". If you frame the opening and then cover the inside faces with $3/4$"-thick trim, the opening will be only $106^1/2$" wide. That's why you need to consider the trim when you lay out your king and jack studs.

Locate the mudsills. Once you've determined the size of your opening (and have taken into account any trim), go ahead and lay out the mudsill locations on your slab, as shown in the bottom left photo. Use a square to make sure the sills are perpendicular to the adjacent walls. Offset the sills as needed for the type of sheathing you'll be using (for more on this, see page 100).

Install the mudsills. When you've located the mudsills, drill holes though them and into the concrete using a hammer drill fitted with a masonry bit, as shown in the bottom right photo. We used concrete screws (Tapcons) to secure the mudsill to the concrete and sandwiched a foam moisture barrier between the two before driving in the screws.

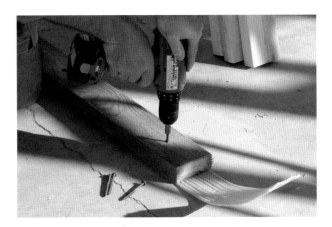

the top plate, and install them at 16" on center. Using the manufacturer's recommended height for the opening, cut a pair of jack studs to length (to support the new header you'll install next), and face-nail these to the king studs.

Install the header. With the jack studs in place, you can build the header. Measure the span between the king studs and cut a pair of 2×6's or 2×8's to this length. Since the combined thickness of the two 2-by pieces is only 3", a piece of $1/2$" plywood or $1/2$" plywood spacers are sandwiched in between the 2-bys to create a $3^1/2$"-thick header. Stack the header parts together with the ends flush, and screw or nail them together. Lift up the header and set it on top of the jack studs. Adjust the header until its face is flush with the front and back edges of the king studs. Then secure the header by driving nails or screws through the king studs and into the ends of the header, as shown in the middle photo.

Install the cripple studs. Measure the distance between the header and the existing header (or top plate), and cut short cripple studs to length. Face-nail one of these to each king stud, and then space the remaining cripple studs 16" on center and toenail them to the header and top plate, as shown in the bottom photo.

Install the wall studs. Now you can cut and install a stud to connect the openings to the house and the king stud to define one side of the opening, as shown in the top left photo. Both of these studs fit between the mudsill and the existing header.

Install the top plate. With the end studs in place, measure between them and cut a top plate to fit. Attach the top plate to the existing header with nails, as shown in the top right photo. Next, measure and cut studs to fit between the mudsill and

horizontal track to the ceiling joists. The track is secured to the ceiling by way of a couple of metal L-brackets on each side of the door. One L-bracket is cut long enough to span two joists and is secured to them with lag screws. Then a vertical L-bracket is connected to the ceiling-mounted bracket and bolted to the horizontal track, as shown in the bottom photo. Repeat this mounting procedure for the other side of the door.

Plumb the vertical track. With all the sections in place, it's time to plumb the vertical track and secure the track completely to the vertical trim piece on the inside face of the door opening. Butt a level up against the track and shift it until it's plumb. Then secure it to the trim with the screws provided, as shown in the top photo.

Install the horizontal track. Now you can install the horizontal track that allows the door to slide up and out of the way. The horizontal track may be bolted to the vertical track or it may simply press-fit onto the top of the vertical track. The easiest way to install the horizontal track it to rest it on your shoulder while you fasten the head bracket of the track to the vertical trim piece with the screws provided, as shown in the middle photo. Repeat this for the remaining horizontal track.

Attach the track to the ceiling. The next step is to attach the unsupported end of the

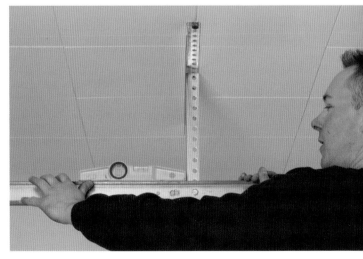

Add bracing. To hold the horizontal track securely and to prevent it from swaying side to side, diagonal braces are run between the ceiling-mounted bracket and the vertical L-bracket, as shown in the top photo. Cut these pieces to length and attach them to the L-brackets with the nuts and bolts provided.

Connect the spring mechanism. All that's left is to add the spring or springs that apply tension to the door so it will be easy to open and close. How you do this will depend on the type of spring or springs your door uses. For the extension springs shown here, the separate springs attach to the back of each L-bracket and are connected to the bottom of the door via a wire rope. This setup applies tension to the bottom of the door to lift it up. Follow the manufacturer's installation instructions to install the springs and wire ropes as shown in the bottom left photo. Adjust them as needed for smooth opening and closing action. Most extension springs also require the installation of a safety containment kit; this prevents a spring from causing damage or injury in case of breakage.

Attach handles to the exterior. At this point the door is installed and you can add any accessories such as decorative or functional handles to the exterior of the door, as shown in the bottom right photo. For the carriage-look door shown here, decorative handles are installed near the center of the door. These handles give the illusion that the door can slide open at its center the way the two halves of an actual carriage door operate.

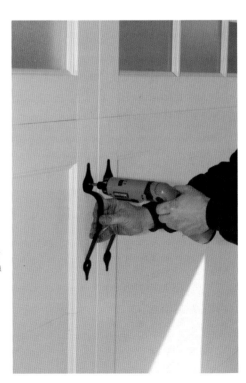

Install the ceiling bracket.

With one end of the opener mounted securely to the header bracket, you can hang the other end—the motor unit. The motor unit attaches to a bracket mounted to the ceiling joists by way of a set of metal L-brackets. The first step here is to locate the ceiling joists with an electronic stud finder. Then cut a piece of L-bracket to span two joists and secure the bracket to the joists with lag bolts, as shown in the top left photo.

Hang the opener. Next, measure and cut L-brackets to connect the motor unit to the ceiling bracket according to the manufacturer's instructions. Have a helper lift up the motor unit so you can secure it to the L-brackets with the bolts provided, as shown in the top right photo.

Connect the door to the track. To connect the opener to the garage door, you'll first have to mount a bracket centered near the top of the door to accept the curved door arm that attaches to the trolley. Once in place, pivot the curved arm up so its end fits into the bracket on the trolley, and secure the arm to the trolley with the clevis pin provided, as shown in the bottom photo.

Install the electrical accessories. The door opener is basically installed now. All that's left is to install and connect the electrical accessories, such as the manual activator and the safety reversing sensors. The manual push button is usually mounted near the entry door so you can open the door manually if you prefer as you step out into the garage. The safety reversing sensors attach to the bottom of the vertical track either with bolts or, as shown in the top photo, by snapping them in place.

Connect the electrical accessories. All of the electrical accessories for most garage door openers operate on low voltage. This means wiring is simple and easy. Just run the cable provided from the manual push button up the wall and over to the motor unit. Run the safety reversing sensor wiring up the wall, over to the center of the door, and across to the motor unit. Attach the wiring to the walls and ceiling with staples or self-adhesive cable clamps. Strip the ends of the wires and connect them to the terminals on the motor unit according to the wiring diagram, as shown in the bottom left photo.

Test for obstructions. With the wiring complete, plug in your motor and test the door operation. Place an obstruction at the bottom of the door between the safety reversing sensors, as shown in the bottom right photo. Press the down button on the opener. The opener should move only about an inch and then stop, indicating that it's unsafe to close the door. The door won't close until the obstruction is removed. Finally, open the door and lay a 2×4 flat on the ground under the door. Close the door; when it hits the 2×4, it should automatically reverse and open.

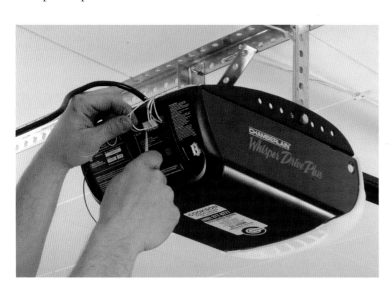

8

STORAGE

"Please—help me organize this mess!" That's the request we hear most often from homeowners about their garages. Overstuffed, cluttered garages are so common that several manufacturers now offer complete storage systems designed to tackle this widespread problem.

In this chapter, well take you through the most popular ways to organize, clean up, and de-clutter a garage. We'll start with RTA, or ready-to-assemble, cabinets and then delve into the many wall-mounted systems available, including Grid Iron, FastTrack, Racor, and Gladiator. For a do-it-yourself option, we'll show you how to make a simple yet sturdy wall-mounted storage system that is fully adjustable. There'll be at least one solution here for all your storage woes.

New Cabinets

TOOLS

- Hammer
- Screwdriver
- Level
- Electronic stud finder (optional)
- Allen wrench set
- Socket set (optional)

For many homeowners, the most-wanted form of storage in a garage is cabinets. It's easy to understand why: Cabinet drawers and doors conceal the contents, so the garage always looks great. Additionally, cabinets offer built-in organization in the form of shelving and drawers. Although you can buy assembled cabinets (like those commonly used for kitchens), they're expensive and require advanced installation skills. A better fit for garage storage is RTA (ready-to-assemble) cabinets, like those shown here made by Hot Rod Garage by Sauder (www.hotrodbysauder.com). These are the cabinets we used for our Mechanic's Dream makeover shown on pages 66–67.

Inspect packages for damage. RTA cabinets are often shipped directly to your door from the manufacturer. When the shipment arrives, before accepting it, check each package carefully for signs of damage, like the torn packaging and scratched panel as shown in the bottom left photo. If you suspect damage, open the package with the delivery person present. Note any broken or bent items on the bill of lading, and contact the distributor or manufacturer for a replacement. Do not uncrate the cabinets until you're ready to assemble them—each cabinet has many parts, and you don't want to lose any or get parts mixed up.

Unpack the contents. When you're ready to assemble the cabinets, set up a work area, including a work surface or saw horses for assembly. Carefully open a cabinet package and pull out the contents, taking the time to group similar parts, as shown in the bottom right photo. Virtually all RTA cabinetmakers clearly label each part, as well as providing excellent assembly instructions. For the small hardware parts, consider using an empty egg carton or a muffin pan to separate and organize

similar parts. Don't discard the packaging until the cabinet is fully assembled, in case you accidentally left a part in the container.

Assemble the cabinet. With all the parts separated and organized, begin following the manufacturer's assembly instructions. Many RTA cabinet go together in a similar manner and use knock-down fittings to secure the parts together; for more on this and typical RTA assembly, see page 162. Once the cabinet is assembled, install any remaining hardware such as feet (as shown in the top photo), handles, pulls, and shelf pins. Repeat for the remaining cabinets.

Position the cabinets. Since most RTA cabinets are made with particleboard or other engineered materials, they tend to be quite heavy. So when it comes time to move the cabinets into their final positions, make sure to have a helper on hand to share the load. Remove as many accessories as you can to lighten the load, such as shelving, drawers, or even cabinet doors. Once you've moved the cabinet into position, you can leave it freestanding (as shown here), attach it to the wall, or attach it to adjacent cabinets for a more stable installation. Most RTA manufacturers provide brackets just for this. If you mount the cabinets to the wall, make sure you attach the brackets to wall studs and take the time to level and plumb the cabinet before securing it to the wall.

Add the cabinet accessories. After securing the cabinets, you can go back and reinstall any accessories you removed to make your work easier, such as the shelving shown in the bottom photo. Level each of the cabinets and adjust the door hinges as needed to square up the cabinet doors and create a uniform gap where the doors meet. Check the manufacturer's assembly sheet for directions on a how to adjust the hinges.

RTA CABINETS

■ With RTA cabinets, all the parts are pre-cut and you assemble the cabinets. The money the manufacturer saves in not assembling the cabinets is passed on to you. Most RTA cabinets have similar hardware—often referred to as "knock-down" hardware because you can loosen the hardware on an assembled cabinet and knock it down for transport. Common knock-down hardware consists of a locking cam that fits in a hole drilled in the face of a cabinet part and a mating bolt that threads into the edge of a cabinet part. Then the cabinet parts are positioned so the bolt fits into the cam; the cam is turned to lock the parts together.

Install the bolts and secure the parts. With the cams in place, the next step is usually to drive the mating bolts into the edge of cabinet parts. When all the cams and bolts have been installed, you position the cabinet parts so the bolts slide into the cams. Then simply rotate the cam with a screwdriver to draw the parts firmly together, as shown in the photo above.

Install the cams. Frequently, one of the first steps to assembling an RTA cabinet is to press the locking cams into the holes drilled in the face of the cabinet parts, as shown in the photo above. These generally are press-fit, and you need to orient each one so the opening in the cam faces the edge of the cabinet part.

Secure parts with screws. An alternative method of securing parts is to use special coarsely threaded screws designed to hold well in particleboard. These screws often require an Allen wrench to drive them in place; many RTA manufacturers include a wrench with the hardware package, as shown in the bottom photo. Drive these screws in until the head just barely sits below the surface of the part.

Wall-Mounted Rack System

I f you're looking for industrial quality in a storage system for your garage, look no further than Grid Iron (www.gidironusa.com). The Grid Iron wall-mounted rack system was inspired by their parent company, which built extremely sturdy merchandise organizers for the retail market. Grid Iron's system is based on unique steel slot-wall panels that feature 1-inch rolled-steel channels. These channels accept a variety of accessories to make customizing a snap. This storage system was by far the most heavy-duty that we used for our makeovers. Although you might expect that we used Grid Iron in a workshop, it's so good-looking that we used it in our living space makeover, shown on pages 72–73. Grid Iron sells startup kits that make ordering what you need simple. We found their ingenious, cantilevered shelving system to be both attractive and sturdy.

TOOLS

• Hammer
• Electronic stud finder
• Level
• Drill with bits
• Screwdriver

Attach the feet.
One of the many things that make the Grid Iron system unique is that although it's a wall-mounted system, Grid Iron designed feet for the bottom of each of their panels to share the load with the wall. So the first thing to do to install a Grid Iron panel is to attach the feet to the bottom of the panel, as shown in the bottom left photo. These feet also let you quickly and easily level the panel before securing it to the wall.

Secure the panels to the wall. Before you attach the panel to the wall, you'll need to locate and mark the wall stud locations with an electronic stud finder. Position the panel on the wall where you want it, and use the adjustable feet to level the panel. Then drill holes through the top of the panel at the wall stud locations and secure the panel to the studs, as shown in the bottom right photo.

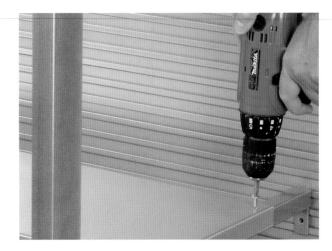

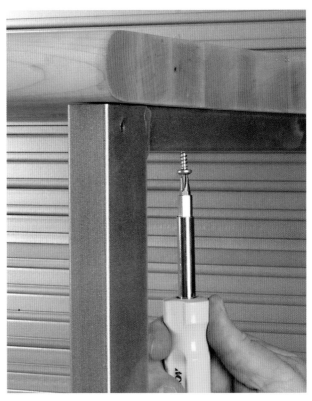

Install the panel connector. Once you have one panel in place, go ahead and install any remaining panels, taking care to level each as you go. To make the already sturdy panels even sturdier, Grid Iron includes a tap-in panel connector with every panel that locks the tops of the panels together. Just position the connector clip over the lips of two adjoining panels and tap it in place with a hammer, as shown in the top left photo.

Install the bench legs and shelf. Grid Iron offers a workbench kit that consists of a pair of welded steel leg assemblies that hook onto the wall panel. The legs are spanned on the bottom by a shelf and on top by a solid-maple worktop. To install a workbench, hook the leg assemblies onto the wall panel at the desired location and connect the two by installing the lower shelf, as shown in the top right photo.

Attach the worktop. The maple worktop rests on top of the leg assemblies and is secured by driving screws up through the tops of the leg assemblies and into the underside of the worktop, as shown in the bottom photo. You'll need to pre-drill holes in the worktop for the screws, so take care to use a depth stop on the drill bit to keep from drilling completely through the top.

as shown in the middle photo. For the all-metal shelf, just hook it on the wall panel and it's ready to go.

Add the remaining accessories. At this point you can add any remaining accessories anywhere on the wall panel or panels by just hooking them onto the panel's lips, as shown in the bottom photo. Grid Iron offers 7" × 16" metal trays, 4" and 8" double-pronged tool hooks, 6" medium- and heavy-duty single hooks, book racks, and small, medium, and large open bins. All of these can be moved around with ease to meet your changing storage needs.

Add the shelving. Grid Iron shelving is a unique two-part system. A bracket hooks onto the wall panel, and a shelf is inserted into the slot in the bracket. This produces a cantilevered shelf that looks almost like it has no visible means of support. Although Grid Iron sells both the shelf bracket and wood shelf in 48" lengths, they can custom-cut both to your specifications (the shelf brackets and shelving shown here are 24" long). In addition to the shelf bracket/shelf system, Grid Iron also offers all-metal shelving that measures 9" × 24".

To install a shelf, simply hook the shelf bracket onto the wall panel at the desired location, as shown in the top photo. Then insert the long edge of the wood shelf into the slot in the shelf bracket,

A Wall Organizer

One of the more popular ways to both add storage to your garage and enhance its looks is to add grooved wall panels like those shown here, made by storeWALL (www.store-wall.com). The storeWALL panels are available in five colors, all with a matte finish. The panels can be installed with their hidden fastener system for a super-clean look. Alternatively, the panels can be screwed directly to wall studs or to drywall-covered studs (as we did here). The panels are made from PVC and come in a variety of widths and lengths. Grooves in the panels accept a variety of accessories (including cabinets) such as those sold by The Accessories Group (www.theaccessoriesgroup.com). Because the grooved panels cover the entire wall, your storage options are extremely flexible.

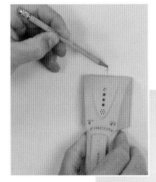

Install the bottom channel. To install the wall panels, start at the bottom and work your way up. Locate the bottom panel the desired distance up from the floor, and secure one end as shown in the bottom right photo. If you're not using storeWALL's hidden fastener system, make sure to use their color-matched screws so the fasteners will be almost invisible.

Locate and mark the wall studs. For the storeWALL panels to be able to support the accessories (and storage items), the panels must be securely fastened to wall studs. Your first order of business is to locate and mark all of the studs, as shown in the inset photo. Then use a level to mark plumb lines at each wall stud location, as shown in the bottom left photo, to make it easy to install the panels.

Level the bottom channel. With one end of the bottom panel attached to a wall stud, set a level on the top edge of the panel and slide the panel up or down until it's level. Then secure the other end of the panel by driving a screw into the nearest wall stud, as shown in the middle photo. Work your way back toward the other end, driving screws in at each stud location. For maximum storage capacity (in terms of weight), drive screws into the wall studs at every slot location on each panel. Repeat for any remaining bottom panels.

Install remaining channels. Once the bottom panels are installed level, the remaining panels go up quickly. That's because the top and bottom edges of each panel snap together via a tongue-and-groove joint. There's a groove on the bottom and a tongue on the top of each panel. Just slip the groove of the next higher panel onto the tongue on the bottom panel. Slide the panel from side to side so that the ends are flush, and screw the panel to the wall studs, as shown in the top photo. To help conceal seams between the butted ends of panels, stagger the panels so the seams don't align. Repeat for any remaining panels.

Cut as needed. It's easy to cut storeWALL panels with standard power tools. A circular saw or miter saw (as shown in the bottom photo), fitted with a carbide-tipped bit, will plow right through a panel, leaving a clean, crisp edge. Interior cutouts, like those for a switch or a receptacle, are easily handled with a saber saw; just make sure to drill access holes for the saber saw blade instead of attempting a plunge cut.

Bin Storage

Locate the studs.

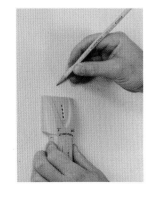

GearWall is easy to install but needs to be securely fastened to wall studs in order to be able to hold its maximum weight capacity of 50 pounds per square foot. Start by locating and marking the wall studs using an electronic stud finder, as shown in the top right photo. For ease of installation it's a good idea to draw a plumb line at each stud location so you'll know where to install screws.

Install the first panel.

Although the GearWall installation instructions direct you to start at the bottom and work up with the panels, we wanted the top panel to be flush with the tops of the workshop windows, so we started at the top and worked our way down. Position a panel on the wall at the desired location and drive in a screw through the slot groove at one end. Use a level and adjust the panel so it's level. Then drive in a screw at the other end into a wall stud, as shown in the bottom photo. For maximum load capacity, drive screws into the studs at every slot groove.

TOOLS

- Electronic stud finder
- Level
- Drill and bits
- Circular or miter saw
- Saber saw (optional)

As part of our Workshop makeover (see pages 70–71), we installed a full wall of Gladiator GearWall panels (www.gladiatorgw.com) and filled them with open bins to organize and store the myriad pieces of hardware in our shop. The bins come with self-adhesive labels so you can quickly locate what you're looking for—no more scrounging through drawers and cabinets to find a much-needed fastener. But Gladiator offers a whole lot more than just bins. They also offer racks, shelving, hooks, and baskets—all of which hook onto their easy-to-install GearWall panels. Additionally, they manufacture coordinated cabinets and even appliances to totally outfit your garage.

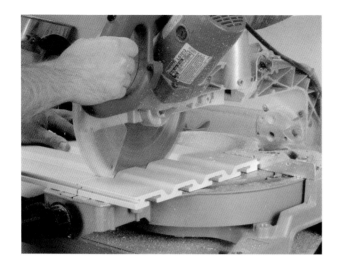

each panel snap together via a tongue-and-groove joint. There's a groove on the bottom and a tongue on the top of each panel. Just slip the groove of the next-higher panel onto the tongue on the bottom panel. Slide the panel from side to side so the ends are flush, and screw the panel to the wall studs, as shown in the bottom photo. To help conceal seams between the butted ends of panels, stagger the panels so the seams don't align.

Cut as needed. You can cut GearWall panels easily with standard power tools. A circular saw or miter saw (as shown in the top photo), fitted with a carbide-tipped bit, will rip right through a panel, leaving a clean, crisp edge. Interior cutouts, like those for a switch or a receptacle, are easily handled with a saber saw; just make sure to drill access holes for the saber saw blade instead of attempting a plunge cut.

Install the remaining panels. After the first panel is installed, go ahead and install the remaining panels. The top and bottom edges of

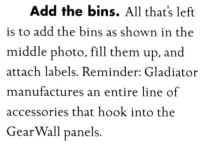

Add the bins. All that's left is to add the bins as shown in the middle photo, fill them up, and attach labels. Reminder: Gladiator manufactures an entire line of accessories that hook into the GearWall panels.

9

ELECTRICAL

For the most part, the electrical improvements you can make as part of a garage makeover are fairly straightforward. Unless you're converting a garage to a workshop and need lots of power, most of the projects are simple and quite do-able by the average do-it-yourselfer.

In this chapter, we'll show you how to upgrade your overhead lighting, and how to add new lighting, switches, and receptacles, using DIY-friendly surface-mount wiring. Then we'll go over other ways to extend circuits, plus how to install the ubiquitous shop lights and how to add under-cabinet lighting to illuminate those all-important work areas. Basically, we'll cover everything you'll need to power up and light up your garage.

Surface-Mount Wiring

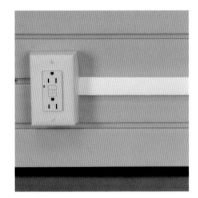

Do you need to add a receptacle or a ceiling light and switch but hesitate to hire an electrician, or to cut holes in your walls to route the new wiring? Consider surface-mount wiring. Surface-mount wiring attaches directly to an existing wall or ceiling; it's available in either metal or plastic. Although the metal type will stand up longer over time, it isn't as easy to work with as the plastic. Both types are paintable, and when painted the same color as the wall, will almost disappear.

To use surface-mount wiring, you'll first need to "tap" into an existing line. Then it's simply a matter of running lengths of metal or plastic channel or "raceway" to the desired location. Raceway is available in a variety of pre-cut lengths, or you can cut it to a custom length using a hacksaw. Connectors, elbows, and boxes complete the run. Then all that's left is to run wire and hook up the new fixtures.

Convert an existing box. To install surface-mount wiring, first locate the receptacle that's closest to where you want your new wiring. Turn off the power to the receptacle at the breaker or fuse panel. Remove the old cover plate and receptacle. Then attach a "starter" box to the electrical box, as shown in the photo at right. A starter box has a large rectangular hole in the plate that attaches to the box; this allows the wiring to pass through into the new box.

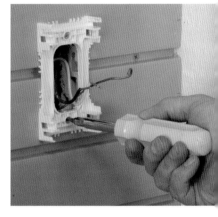

Install the raceway. Now you're ready to measure and cut lengths of raceway to reach the destination of the new box. Press-fit connectors and inside and outside elbows make this an easy task. Just make sure to subtract the length of the connector from the raceway before you cut it to length. Attach the raceway to the wall by screwing directly into studs, or drill holes for plastic anchors, as shown in the bottom photo.

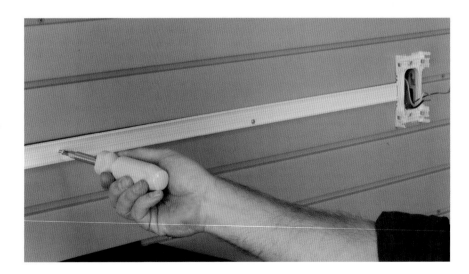

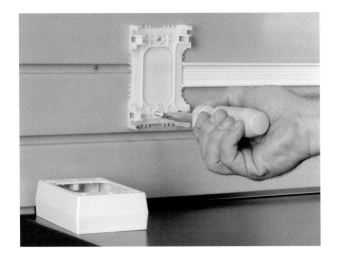

Add the boxes. Just like the raceway, surface-mount boxes are attached to the wall either by screwing into studs or by drilling holes for plastic anchors. To use plastic anchors, position the back plate of the box where you want it and make a mark through the mounting holes in the back. Then drill holes, insert the plastic anchors, and screw the back plate to the wall, as shown in the top photo.

Run the wiring. It's simple to run the wiring through surface-mount raceways. All you have to do is cut the wire to length plus 6" extra on each end for your electrical connections. Then place it in the raceway and thread the ends into the boxes, as shown in the bottom photo. Most surface-mount systems come with snap-in flexible plastic clips that fit inside the track to hold the wiring in place. With the wiring in place, you can install the covers onto the raceway to conceal and protect the wiring. Both the metal and plastic varieties simply snap onto the raceway. After you've installed all the covers on the raceways, you can add the covers to the electrical boxes. Here again, these simply snap into place (bottom inset photo).

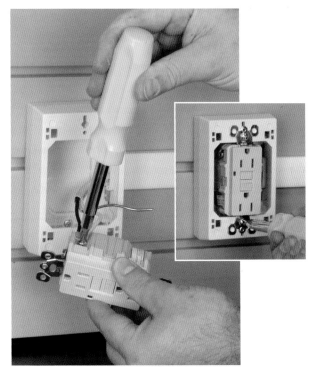

Wire the receptacle or switch. Strip the ends of the wires you've run as needed to make your electrical connections. Connect the wiring to the receptacle, as shown in the middle photo. When done, push the wiring back into the surface-mount box and screw the receptacle to the new box, as shown in the middle inset photo above. If you're installing receptacles or switches, you'll want to wire these now, too. Finally, you can add any cover plates to the surface-mount boxes. If you've installed metal raceways, you may need to secure the raceways to the wall with metal straps that fit over the raceway. In most cases, you'll secure these to the wall with plastic anchors.

Under-Cabinet Lighting

you're mounting it to and the size of the worktop. Try plugging in the light and holding it in place under the cabinet or shelf as shown in the top right photo. Move it around to provide the best light.

Mark the mounting hole locations.
When you've determined the best position for the light, locate and mark the holes for the mounting hardware. Some lighting manufacturers provide a template for this. With other lamps (like the one shown here), the light itself is the template. Hold it in place and mark up through the mounting holes in the lamp on the underside of the shelf or cabinet, as shown in the bottom photo.

TOOLS

- Screwdriver
- Electric drill and bits

If your makeover includes shelving or cabinets that hang over a workbench or other work surface, you'll want to install under-cabinet lighting to illuminate the work area. Under-cabinet lighting can be as simple as installing a single strip light underneath the overhead cabinets, or as complex as adding a series of puck lights.

Locate the best position for the light.
Although you can mount an under-cabinet light anywhere underneath a cabinet, most manufacturers recommend locating the strip as close to the front of the cabinet as possible to create the best coverage. It all depends on the cabinet or shelf

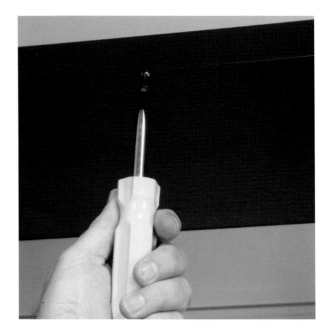

Mount the light. Mate the keyhole-shaped slots in the underside of the light fixture with the screws you just installed, and then slide the fixture over in the slots in the fixture to lock it in place (bottom photo). Most under-cabinet fixtures are designed to plug into a wall receptacle. Halogen fixtures typically require adding a low-voltage transformer that plugs into a standard receptacle. Note: If the under-cabinet lights you've mounted are visible at eye level, install a concealment strip to hide the strip and prevent glare. This strip can be just a 1" to 2" strip of wood or molding nailed to the front edge and finished to match the cabinet or shelf.

Drill the mounting holes. Set the lamp aside and, using the recommended-sized bit, drill pilot holes for the mounting screws in the underside of the shelf or cabinet, as shown in the top left photo.

Install the mounting screws. Most under-cabinet lights come with fasteners. Drive these up into the underside of the cabinet or shelf, as shown in the top right photo. For puck-style lights, the mounting screws are typically driven up through a plastic base for the puck; then the puck snaps into the base.

Index

METRIC EQUIVALENCY CHART

Inches to millimeters and centimeters

inches	mm	cm	inches	cm	inches	cm
1/8	3	0.3	9	22.9	30	76.2
1/4	6	0.6	10	25.4	31	78.7
3/8	10	1.0	11	27.9	32	81.3
1/2	13	1.3	12	30.5	33	83.8
5/8	16	1.6	13	33.0	34	86.4
3/4	19	1.9	14	35.6	35	88.9
7/8	22	2.2	15	38.1	36	91.4
1	25	2.5	16	40.6	37	94.0
1 1/4	32	3.2	17	43.2	38	96.5
1 1/2	38	3.8	18	45.7	39	99.1
1 3/4	44	4.4	19	48.3	40	101.6
2	51	5.1	20	50.8	41	104.1
2 1/2	64	6.4	21	53.3	42	106.7
3	76	7.6	22	55.9	43	109.2
3 1/2	89	8.9	23	58.4	44	111.8
4	102	10.2	24	61.0	45	114.3
4 1/2	114	11.4	25	63.5	46	116.8
5	127	12.7	26	66.0	47	119.4
6	152	15.2	27	68.6	48	121.9
7	178	17.8	28	71.1	49	124.5
8	203	20.3	29	73.7	50	127.0

mm = millimeters   cm = centimeters

Photo credits

Alcoa (www.alcoa.com): page 10 (middle).
All-American (www.allamericandoors.com):
    page 22 (bottom right).
Amarr (www.amarr.com): page 12 (all), page
    47 (middle).
Armstrong (www.armstrong.com): page 23
    (top right, middle and bottom), page 28
    (top), page 29 (top), page 120, page 128.
Andersen (www.andersenwindows.com):
    page 20 (both middle), page 38 (all), page
    39 (top and middle).
Better Life Technology (www.bltllc.com):
    page 31 (all), page 95 (bottom).
CertainTeed (www.certainteed.com): page 22
    (top and bottom left), page 36 (both
    bottom), page 107 (all).
Chamberlain (www.chamberlain.com):
    page 42 (all).
Clopay (www.clopaydoor.com): page 10 (top),
    page 13 (top), page 16 (all), page 17 (all),
    page 26, page 40 (all), page 47 (top left).

Eldorado Stone (www.eldoradostone.com):
    page 22 (middle).
Fly Away AgriProducts (www.flyawayagri.com):
    page 35 (all bottom).
Grid Iron (www.gridironusa.com): page 24
    (top), page 45 (middle).
JELD-WEN (www.jeld-wen.com): page 20
    (top), page 134.
Mohawk (www.mohawkind.com): page 28
    (bottom), page 29 (middle).
MonierLifetile (www.monierlifetile.com): page
    11 (top), page 13 (middle).
ODL (www.odl.com): page 18 (top).
Owens Corning (www.owens-corning.com):
    page 13 (bottom).
RaceDeck (www.racedeck.com): page 23 (top
    left), page 91 (bottom).
Racor (www.racorinc.com): page 24 (bottom),
    page 45 (top), page 176 (bottom left).
Raynor (www.raynor.com): page 47 (bottom).

Rubbermaid (www.rubbermaid.com): page
    44 (bottom and inset), page 45 (bottom).
Rust-Oleum (www.rustoleum.com): page 30
    (top), page 88 (top).
Sauder (www.hotrodbysauder.com): page 43
    (all), page 158.
Solatube (wwwsolatube.com): page 20
    (bottom).
Southern Pine (www.southernpine.com):
    page 58.
storeWALL (www.storewall.com): page 44
    (top and inset).
Therma-Tru (www.thermatru.com): page 18
    (middle).
Triton Products (www.tritonproducts.com):
    page 117 (top).
Wayne-Dalton (www.wayne-dalton.com):
    page 6, page 10 (bottom), page 11 (middle
    and bottom), pages 18–19 (bottom), page
    48, page 180.
Wilsonart (www.wilsonart.com): page 29
    (both bottom).